Control: From Time Management, Willpower and Persuasion to a Successful Startup with Less Than $100

Benjamin Rich

Copyright © 2019 Benjamin Rich

All rights reserved.

ISBN: 9781712427910

An eye-opening book that reveals how to start a profitable business through passion and continuous innovation in a short time.

CONTENTS

	Introduction	Pg 1
1	The Passion	Pg 4
2	Time, Money and Experience	Pg 21
3	The Willpower	Pg 27
4	Value and Persuasion	Pg 36
5	Startup Definition	Pg 51
6	Validation Process	Pg 53
7	The Plan	Pg 67
8	The Best Price	Pg 78
9	The Funds	Pg 83

INTRODUCTION

This book is divided into two parts which can also be addressed independently. In the first part we will talk about the mental approach, an extremely undervalued topic. The difference between a successful startup and a bankruptcy lies precisely in the mental approach of its founder. The logical and motivational approach allows us to arrive where others, even if apparently more brilliant, do not arrive.

In the second part we will see, in practice, how to start a startup with less than $100.

With $100 you can certainly start a startup, this is correct. With this book I will show you and explain it in detail.

Is this the case where a young man with a brilliant idea meets a stroke of luck? No, unfortunately this is not the reality. Just think of any person who has succeeded in the business world. A brilliant idea and a stroke of luck is not enough. The situation needs to be controlled. You control the situation when you know what you are doing. Also, if by mistake you have found something really powerful, but you can't manage it as a business, you're out.

Maybe someone else will come, more "awake" than you, and succeed in "stealing" the idea. So how do we become "awake" enough to have control over our ideas and make them productive?

An old Chinese proverb says: "A theory vessel is not worth as much as a drop of practice". There is no book or course worth more than a hands-on approach.

When you have built experience in the field, then you will finally be able to control your idea and make it bear fruit. To sum up: you need more control (therefore experience) than luck if you want to actually carry out a successful startup for more than a few weeks.

It is an evolutionary path. One cannot begin by saying: "Tomorrow I will start my successful startup!"

There's nothing useful to be learned from those who say: "Start this type of business, I guarantee you will earn 5 figures a month!". Or rather, there may certainly be interesting ideas, but experience is not taught. So, ideas are welcome, but need to be accompanied by experience to put them into action.

Suppose you have an idea: "Selling a book on Amazon where you explain to people something you are particularly good at".

If you start with 0 experience, even with $2000, you probably won't be doing anything productive. Certainly, if you have no experience, you must study the process and layout of a book, making the cover, the "page ranking" for books on Amazon, the conditions that the content of your book must respect, and so on. Until you have full control of all these things, you won't go far. Also consider that all these and other problems will appear unexpectedly, one after the other, in your path, because initially you are unaware of their existence. For anyone who approaches a new business, initially the goal seems to be a few hours of work. Then, when we start, we get the impression that the more we go forward, the further the goal becomes and a few hours of work are transformed into months.

You can have control of your idea when you know what you are doing.

Behind phenomena like Facebook, there is not only a brilliant idea, but also a lot of work and experience. It is true that Apple started from a garage, but those who worked on it did not improvise. Things do not come by themselves unless we want them.

We were saying that this is an evolutionary path. A path that will start from your passions (the most precious things you have) and will allow you to gain experience incrementally. Before arriving at the winning idea, you will pass for other simpler and less ambitious ideas that you will need to gain more and more control over.

If you think you have a winning idea (I don't doubt that it is), I invite you to try to implement it and be successful without experience. Maybe you can, but it's very likely that you fail. Make the most of this failure and understand the importance of the experience. We are ready to learn how to make a lot of useful experience in a short time and, above all, doing something we like.

1 THE PASSION

The following section of this book, as I already mentioned, starts far away from the fields of business and strategy. You can feel a bit lost reading the first pages.

Don't worry, the pieces of the puzzle will soon be composed.

Ok, here we go, where do we start? I have already mentioned it: from passion. If you already have an idea or if you are still looking for it, it does not matter. If there is no passion there is no fuel to go on.

The goal is to design our evolutionary path in the best way for us. To do this we must comply with what we like to do. Attention: what we like is not always the same as what we do well! It takes a lot of honesty to separate these two categories. What we like does not weigh on us and we are automatically led to know more and more about it. In this way we exploit our natural propulsion to build our business experience.

Having to do a deep analysis within ourselves, let's take a closer look at the passion.

"Working to earn" has become the standard to which all, young and old, aspire to the most, but not by their own will. Today, young people are fighting for jobs with few outlets and that do not provide, in addition to adequate remuneration, even the skills that make them "expendable" on the labor market. In general, these are "mechanical" and repetitive jobs that offer no opportunity for improvement and personal/professional development. We realize that the malaise of young people who do not find a job translates into the mistaken belief that they are not enough to be able to do something. This serious conviction has, subsequently, a domino effect on all their psychic system, with the collapse of self-esteem.

Thus, there is the total collapse of that mental structure capable of supporting people during the most demanding and productive processes (such as becoming an entrepreneur).

The only way to succeed is to love your work. Passion gives you that motivational drive that can make you work for hours and hours without realizing it. Those who work for passion are as if they were playing a hobby. He never gets tired and gets better and better. That is why it is essential, from whatever point you are leaving, to work for passion. Surely with a scenario like the one we are traveling in, working for passion seems like a mirage but it is not. Indeed, it is the smartest thing to do.

Success has almost always come to those who have followed their own interests and passions. The great entrepreneurs often have in common the fact that they have created (and worked for) something they loved to do. These characters love their work, they love what they do, and it was precisely this love that brought them to where they are today, and that made them become the people they became. Many of them started from the bottom and they too encountered a thousand (and one) difficulties, but did not give up. Their passions were stronger than anything. One of the most important rules of success is that: "success is the natural consequence of love". Love for one's work, for one's passions, love for what one does.

"Passion is the oxygen of the soul." - Bill Butler

They made us believe that these motivations are right and founded, but if we answer, with courage and honesty, a "no" to the question "am I happy doing what I do?" that means we have to change something. Life is precious and unfortunately also ephemeral and very short. You must always remember that a day spent not working towards your dreams and your goals is a lost day. What matters is doing something you love and loving what you do. Only in this way will you give "more life to the days and no more days to life" and you will be happy.

I propose you a set of rules (things to do, things to remember, actions, behaviors, ways of thinking) that have produced winning results. These rules therefore, if assimilated, followed, and made their own, allow you to replicate the same results:

Working for passion means working for love. Work for love. Success will come (this is the hardest in my opinion).

If you work for passion you will have the opportunity to earn great wealth.

Boring, repetitive and out of work means the death of creativity and enthusiasm. You have two options: work to earn or work for passion.

Successful people work with passion.

If you are not happy with your current job, ask yourself why and then act accordingly.

This set of rules is a small and simple piece of information that can drastically change your life if you assimilate it and make it your own.

Many may have a question: "ok, but how do I understand what I really like doing? How can I tell if I've really identified my passion?"

I certainly won't tell you what's best for you, I just want to help you in understanding it.

Only you can find this answer.

Always remember that happiness is your big goal.

Many make the mistake of thinking: today I find any job, then tomorrow, when I own more money, I will start doing what I really like.

But if you don't know what job to do, you will never find the right job for you.

All these people are still waiting for that tomorrow.

Do you want to join them?

Often the most difficult question is this: what do you like to do in life? What are you passionate about?

It seems absurd to many that it is a difficult question, yet it really puts us in a struggle.

Do you know what you really love doing?

It is difficult to understand what work to do in your life without understanding what interests you.

It may not be true that in your past experiences there are passions, but it is better to check before discarding them!

I'm not interested in what you did, I'm more interested in what the experience gave you, because you did it and how it changed you.

But let's go in order.

Start writing all the jobs you've done so far in your life.

Since we are looking for your way, take them all into consideration.

Both those that lasted for years and those of a few months, whether you were regular or without a contract.

In short, it lists all the times you've worked; that they paid you to do something.

Now you have to ask yourself a series of questions for each job, and you have to do them very calmly, giving yourself all the time you need to answer.

Small premise: how to understand what to do in life is a crucial step because you could invest a lot of future years into this activity.

Do not rush.

That being said, here are the questions to ask for each of your professional experiences:

1. Why did you do that job? Just for the money or for some other reason? It doesn't matter if it's professional, you're interested in understanding more about your choice.

2. What did you like about that experience? They could also be details of little value or marginal things.

3. Why did you like these things? Why not others?

4. What amused or enthused you? Were there moments, activities, situations that you lived with enthusiasm, with a great desire to do? Forget if the behaviors of others were negative, what did you enjoy?

5. For what reason? Some things excite you or entertain you, others don't. What was the difference? What changed?

Answer all the questions, one work experience at a time.

Do not rush it, do not respond superficially.

Give yourself time, think about it calmly, reflect, evaluate your answers, then read them again.

Realize that you are doing something fundamental, which if done right will lead you to one of the most important answers in your life.

Imagine that it is your grandmother, or an elderly gentleman, who reads these answers: would he understand your motives and your feelings?

Would he know why you liked one thing rather than another?

Try to be clear, much precision is essential.

Write the questions on a piece of paper and go to a quiet place where you can think about it and think about it calmly.

Even if you spend multiple days, that's fine.

You need clear and precise answers.

Control – Benjamin Rich

Consider that you don't care much about the work itself.

It must interest you why, even a job you didn't like, could excite you in some situation.

When you understand this, you are better understanding your tastes, what you like and what you don't like.

The work itself is not important, but the reason why you do it, what excites you, the circumstances in which it absorbs you completely, when passion takes over.

Maybe you have had bad experiences, but some positive details you might find there too, and you actually care about that detail.

To understand what to do in life, you cannot settle for a "role" to cover.

You have to find out what you're passionate about, and often we find clues everywhere, even while we do things that don't interest us at all.

School setting.

Come on, we spend a lot of years, we study, we hear, we listen to so many things, we experience: that would have to do something, don't you think?

Again, make a list of the schools you have attended.

If you studied law, you may want to become a singer, who cares?

You have to go looking, once again, for the sparks of passion and interest, the enthusiasm, that I am sure you will have experienced from time to time in your study path.

Maybe you didn't like the school you did or the professional opportunities it offers don't interest you.

It's fine.

Remember that it does not matter what is written on that piece of paper that you keep attached to the wall.

It is important what you have learned, what experience has allowed you to do, how you have changed.

Here are some questions to guide you in this second phase.

1. Were there any subjects you liked? Even if they were those that lasted one or two hours a week. Identify what intrigued and interested you, even if marginal.

2. What were the best experiences? You have been studying for several years, and maybe you still do it, but there is certainly something special left thanks to some moments. Which ones are they? And why did they stay in it?

3. Perhaps all the things studied were useless and boring but won't there be some topic, some pages of a book, or a sub-chapter that you have appreciated in these years? Strive to find what you did like, what did you do that for?

4. What impressed you about your journey? Extracurricular experiences? Any teachers who left you something positive?

Try to capture all the good you have found and understand why you like it. Consider it positive and remember it with affection.

The same rule applies as before: you have to look for the slightest indication of passion, enthusiasm and interest.

Imagine these answers, along with all the ones you will come up with by reading the next pages, like pieces of a puzzle: the more you have, the easier it will be to recreate the image on the box.

The last phase of this quest for pieces of your puzzle: what do you like to do in your spare time?

This is perhaps a much simpler question.

How do you spend your free time?

It is also the most important question, because maybe we often study and work as a necessity, perhaps not even too freely chosen.

In our free time, however, we do what really interests us and we dedicate ourselves to things that we really like.

Think of all the hobbies you've cultivated in the past, not just the current ones.

As we did before, write them all and ask yourself the next questions for each of them.

1. Why do you have this passion? What do you like, exactly?

2. Which are the aspects that excite you the most? Why these and not others?

3. If you had to convince kids to dedicate themselves to this passion of yours, how would you motivate them? What could excite them?

4. If you could no longer devote time to it, what would you miss most?

5. What could happen to make you lose enthusiasm?

Imagine what would change in you, or in the things you do, to make you may lose interest.

I remind you that, even in this case, it is not important what you are doing in free time, but the reasons why you do it.

Maybe in free time I like to chop wood, but it's certainly not what I want to do in life.

How to understand what to do in life? How to find your own way?

It is obvious that you do not ask yourself this question to understand how to spend Saturday afternoons, but how to occupy most of your time.

Let's talk about work, then.

Work is understood as that activity which must be something you are passionate about, which gives you the opportunity to make a difference and give you satisfaction.

There are many things you like to do. Certainly with some time and sincere answers you will find even more.

But the real, deep passion that must become your work is something else.

Having said this, we must complete our orientation and understand how to recognize a true passion from simple interests.

Maybe you have in mind a profession that you like, but you don't have the certainty that it is the right thing for you.

In this case you need to understand what it means in terms of concrete activities.

The idea of the doctor in a hospital, for example, is fascinating, also thanks to television. But, if you become the profession you have in mind, ask yourself:

1. What do you do in that role?

2. What are the rhythms of that work?

3. What would you do every day, every week?

4. Who are you dealing with? What kind of problems do you have to solve?

5. What knowledge do you need to do it? How can you get it? How long does it take and how much does it cost?

6. What are the side effects? The inconvenient parts of this activity? The unpleasant or annoying aspects?

You must have precise answers to all these questions.

Do you have friends who do that job? Great, talk to them and find out what they do.

Do you have the opportunity to spend some time with them and see them at work? Even better.

If you don't know anyone, you could go to industry websites and forums, read newspapers aimed at those professionals, or contact someone via LinkedIn and ask for information.

Use other social networks to ask questions to those who carry out that profession, or do research on Google.

The important thing is that you understand what it means to do that job.

No theory or hearsay.

Whether you have a job in mind or not, the important thing is that you are able to understand what you would like to do.

It doesn't matter if it's something that exists or if what you'd like is normally divided between more professions.

You have to understand what you're passionate about. This is the most important thing.

You have information taken from your previous jobs (and perhaps from the current one), from what you have studied and from the interests to which you dedicate your free time.

Maybe you have also gathered a lot of information on some jobs that you like.

Your goal is to put these elements together and define what you'd like to do.

Let's clarify first that passion and employment are different things.

If you like music, it doesn't mean you have to be a singer, or a musician.

You could prefer composition, writing music for video games, or becoming a music critic.

What interests you is to understand what you like to do, what you are passionate about.

Don't think about a particular profession. The question "what job to do?" will come later. Right now it would hinder you and nothing else.

The risk is to get caught up in labels and narrow categories which throttle your true passion.

Don't mind the work you could do.

Thinking about your typical day, what would you like to do?

Go into detail, make a real daily program made of practical activities, commitments and specific things you do.

How do you imagine your work?

Do this exercise without limiting yourself to the tasks of this or that profession. Get out of the box.

Imagine having to invent a new job (if you are reading this book it is probably what you will do):

1. What tasks do you perform during the day? What takes up your time?

2. What goals do you have to reach each evening, every week or every month?

3. What tools do you want to use to do it?

4. How will you use them? How do you interact with others in your work?

5. Who do you contact? Who would your customers be?

6. What do you do for them? Why do they ask for help from you?

7. If there are people who do something similar, what is the difference between you and them?

8. What would you be unique in?

Write the answers to these questions but remember: don't think about a normal job.

Don't think about what the lawyer does, rather than the carpenter, the electrician or the doctor.

Don't answer these questions by thinking about what the saleswoman, the waiter or the receptionist does.

Create answers that are yours.

Here are some more clues you will need:

Do you prefer to organize your time independently?

Do you want a paid job, to be an employee, or self-employed, or a freelancer?

These are two other really important elements.

Once you have finished this process, you are facing not an occupation, but a way in which you could commit yourself every day. Something for which it is worth laboring and working.

But is it really your passion?

Something that you will have the strength to transform into your work, concretely?

You know what you want to do, you have an idea of how you want to spend your time.

The first thing to do is to answer this question: is it something useful and positive for others?

If the answer is no, forget it.

Do you remember that we started from a basic consideration? Yes: you want to be happy.

Good.

Never forget it.

And I guarantee you that you can't be happy, really, if you don't act with love, even through your work.

Imagine doing what looks fantastic to you today, even in 20 years.

Not only that, imagine you get up every morning for 20 years, to always take care of the same thing.

Of course, consider that any job will always be new. The problems you face change, your approach or the people you deal with.

In general, though, do you see yourself doing the same job all this time?

How do you imagine yourself in 20 or 30 years?

Consider a very important thing: I'm not telling you that what you choose must do it for your whole life. Times change and so does work

The point is: don't start a journey if you don't intend to go all the way.

It wouldn't make sense, it wouldn't motivate you when you encounter difficulties and obstacles.

It wouldn't be a passion if in a few years you think you're annoyed!

Reflect calmly and try to understand if it is really something that would excite you even in 10 or 20 years.

Would you be willing to work for free?

Ok, no economic problem, you have everything you need to live in dignity.

You get up every morning and spend all your time for free. Your passion is true if you are willing to work for free, every day, forever.

I'm not saying a few weeks or for a trial period.

I'm saying forever.

Working for free is essential. If you don't want to do it, it means that you don't really love this job.

If you want to be happy you have to make one that you like regardless of everything.

You have to get up with enthusiasm every morning because you can't wait to get started.

Face any problem with serenity, because you like to solve those kinds of problems.

It doesn't have to be money to motivate you. That would be a disaster.

It must be passion.

Who pays you to grow a hobby?

Nobody.

Love, that's what drives us to do better things and makes us happy.

You have to love what you do and do it just because you love it.

Would you ever stop doing something you like because you have reached a certain age?

In retirement you go there because the work has tired you. You don't want to get up early and it annoys you. You can't stand the problems to face anymore, you want to do something else.

If you like painting, I don't think you will stop because you are of retirement age.

You like it, you don't want to stop.

It must be something you would never retire to and not even on vacation.

I tell you clearly: resting is ok but wanting to leave for two weeks and not being able to wait for the holidays to start is something different.

Control – Benjamin Rich

When you want to stop working it means you don't love what you do.

Obviously, we do not confuse passion with the obsession of those who cannot stop working.

They are different things.

But if you have a passion and you're on vacation, don't paint, don't play or don't dance because you're on vacation?

It would be ridiculous; indeed, it is just the opposite: we are waiting for holidays to do the things we really love.

You do it because you like it, and don't stop because you like it.

Simple.

Consider that you are not looking for just what job to do, but how to spend the time at your disposal.

Something that only you can do. Wait for yourself.

Having a passion so great that you want to create it for free, forever, without holidays, or for reasons other than love for what you do, is a gift.

A gift that cannot be ignored and that helps to understand how to find one's way.

Find it, it's one of the most important things, because it's not a job, it's your way.

If so, try and experiment.

Often you have the idea that that job would be fantastic or that another would be horrible.

Now you have clearer ideas, or better, you know how to really enlighten them.

Carefully follow the ideas you have read, answer all the questions, and take time to find out who you are and what you want, what you like.

Don't be in a hurry, what you are looking for is a very important answer.

First, though, you must have this answer.

Think about it calmly: would you do it for free, forever?

If the answer is yes, a convinced yes, you have discovered what to do.

If what you have found has nothing to do with the world of business or startups, it doesn't matter. If you are reading this book, you probably had certain intentions and plans. If you understand that your way is another, follow your natural path, otherwise you risk throwing away your time.

Once we understand what we are passionate about, we have already outlined the environment in which our evolution will take place.

Now that we know what our goal will be, we must define the starting point and the evolutionary path that will lead us to the goal.

2 TIME, MONEY AND EXPERIENCE

Therefore, do it out of passion not for money. Of course, to survive you need some money, but it's not money that makes the difference in your life. It is simply overrated and much less influential than what you think. If you are in possession of this book, perhaps one of the reasons that pushes you to consult the contents is money. Many people who set money as their goal are not very rational in identifying the deep reasons that lead them to set themselves this goal. They often let themselves be carried away by a common idea, but without having carried out a critical analysis on the reasons behind their choice. I want to offer you some thoughts, from which my position regarding this problem will clearly emerge. I want you to be convinced of your motivation and your goals. We have already seen how important the concept of control is and not even the profound knowledge of its objectives is an exception.

What really differentiates millionaires from all others is not luxury cars and pool villas. Their most precious asset is not money, but the time they have available to do what they want.

Money itself does not make people happy. If we believe it, it's because we have been convinced that having lots of money means having more time to dedicate to ourselves, our loved ones and our passions.

From childhood we are led to believe that money makes happiness. We pour out our desire to feel good about objects, as if they were actually the origin of well-being.

We grow convinced that things make us happy and consequently we become obsessed with money. Because without money we can't buy all those objects that we see everywhere: on television, on social networks, in newspapers, and so on.

From an early age, we convince ourselves that money is the most precious asset.

For many, the equation "+ money = + things = + happiness" is an untouchable truth.

The problem is that all of us, sooner or later, find ourselves at a point in our lives in which money has absolutely nothing. And when we get there, we realize that there is a much more valuable asset.

There is nothing more democratic than death.

At that moment, your bank account and the objects you have accumulated are absolutely worthless. Each of us takes different paths of life, but when we reach that point, we are all the same.

And with an almost absolute certainty, I can say that any person about to die thinks that the most important asset is not money, but time. If he could, he would give away all he has to have more time.

Money can accumulate and lose. You can be richer or poorer every day. Objects are bought, broken and thrown to buy others.

You can always find a way to increase your money or assets, but there is no way to increase your time.

From an early age we are stimulated to pursue many things, but not time.

We are told to study to get a good job, which allows us to buy a big house and a powerful car. When we become adults, that instinct is still within us, stronger than ever. In fact we do not choose the work we like most, but the one that pays the best.

The false myth, that wants material wealth equal to happiness, infects us as children and pushes us when we grow up to never say no in front of the opportunity to make money. Even when we don't need it. Even at the expense of our relationships, our passions and our health.

That's why I talk about passion. I'm certainly not talking about living in poverty, or anything like that. It is necessary to distinguish well between passion and money, they are two very different objectives. With passion, one simply gives meaning to one's life, with money you're just chasing a shadow without ever getting to something that really matters.

Every time I asked "what was the happiest moment of your life?" I received all kinds of answers, but in no case was I told "when I bought the last iPhone" or "when I received my salary".

I was told "when I graduated", or "when I made the journey to Santiago" or "when I became a mother".

To find out the value of a year, ask a student who has failed the final exam. To find out the value of a month, ask a mother who gave birth to a child too soon. To find out the value of a week, ask the editor of a weekly magazine. To find out the value of an hour, ask the lovers who are waiting to see each other. To find out the value of a minute, ask someone who has just missed the train, bus or plane. To find out the value of a second, ask someone who has survived an accident. To find out the value of a millisecond, ask an athlete who won the silver medal at the Olympics.

Time waits for no one.

We were inculcated with the misconception that we must follow the traditional career path by working 50 hours a week to receive a fixed salary. Get in the office early, stay up late and even be available over the weekend - then maybe, just maybe, one day we'll get a raise.

As long as you trade time for money, your income will always be limited.

The first reason is obvious: there are only 24 hours in a day to devote to pursuing money. And most of us need eight hours to sleep, two hours to get to and from work and two to four hours, in all, to cook, eat, take care of hygiene, relax and spend time with friends and the family.

Speaking in materialistic terms, this leaves us with only 10-12 hours to exchange for money. That's all.

There is no rule that says that to make X dollars, we have to work Y hours.

So, think of exchanging value for money, not time. Think about what you can create and that has value for others, and how you can bestow that VALUE.

Jim Rohn said:

"We get paid for bringing value to the marketplace."

In this case we are talking about functional value

Very often the price is determined not based on the economic value of a product, but on the basis of the value we attribute to the function performed: the functional value of a product will be given to us by how much we are willing to pay for the function that a product performs for us at the time of purchase.

In other words, the value is related to the satisfaction of our need. We will talk about value in a more in-depth manner later.

So even if you don't have so much money to invest in your ideas, if you have the right time, you can get anywhere. As we have seen, time is the most powerful and effective element that can be used. It is not necessary to dispose of so much time, but of that strictly necessary to make a good idea work. The alchemic combination that generates profit is therefore time + good idea + experience (by "good idea" we mean an idea able to create value).

Having made this necessary clarification, you remain with your goal, without distractions like money, guilt or other nonsense.

The starting point is called a "very simple idea".

Now: how do you get a good idea?

Now you don't have enough experience to give substance to an idea even of medium complexity.

The world and its needs are changing ever more quickly, so when you have given birth to a brilliant idea, it will probably be too late. By the time you are developing it, it will have already lost almost all its effectiveness and you will end up having nothing.

Control – Benjamin Rich

Our control craze requires us to immediately look for a definitive situation, but the times involved do not allow it. Too strict a coherence, especially at the beginning, can greatly damage those who approach the business world. In reality, it is not necessary to wait long before having very important results, the point is that probably these results will not be obtained through the way that they had initially thought. It is good to start with something small, maybe something you can already control.

If you can be humble and flexible in this sense, you will see that you will have incredible benefits from this approach.

Among all the very simple ideas I can have, which one do I choose, how do I find myself?

You already know how your dream startup will look, we already understood that a few pages ago.

Now make a list of all the things you know how to do and think about how to use them to do something that makes you earn. Think about your destination and use the skills you already have to get access to the experiences, notions and information you think you will need for your final project.

For example: my starting point is: I can cook quite well. My goal is: I want to be an actor.

I can open a YouTube channel where I talk about cooking recipes to enhance my mastery of performance and confidence with the camera. Or I can be a cook in a theater structure to have access to an interesting environment.

Then it makes no sense to worry. It is enough to have a small, even mediocre idea and carry it on until the possibility of moving to the next idea arises. The experience will transform the starting point several times into better and better projects until it leads to the goal. You will go from idea to idea getting closer to the goal more and more, going to build the experience you need to have control over every area of your final project.

How can I tell when I have total control of my first idea, and can I start the next one?

It will never be too late, because even the most banal idea really has a colossal number of things to teach. On the other hand, it is stupid to get lost in the details and give up on evolving when we are already on the go. The right time to move to a new idea is determined in a really simple, almost disappointing way: "when you feel ready". If you can't understand if you're ready, you can try! You will understand if the moment has arrived based on the success or the success of the idea you want to implement. It is a concept that is as simple as it is unsettling.

Obviously, it must be an idea that allows us to learn something useful or better to get even closer than before to the work that represents our goal.

Returning to the previous example: if you had chosen to open a YouTube channel on how to cook as a first idea, a second step could be to hold live cooking lessons, as more fluency is needed than being alone behind a camera.

In this case, when I feel quite experienced in the field of video lessons on YouTube, I can gradually move on to this new idea. The degree of confidence needed to move from one idea to another obviously depends on the two ideas. Certainly, the practice is the greatest teacher. These are gradual evolutionary transition paths, so nothing happens if you have overestimated your capacity and you are not yet up to it. Let's say you don't leave a step until your foot is resting well on the one above. If you are still not able to move on to the next step, there is no problem: the important thing is to continue to accumulate experience and not get involved by failures.

What will send you forward despite everything is called will power. The will power deserves to be thoroughly investigated because, without a strong and well-trained will power, it is not possible to reach our goal.

3 THE WILLPOWER

There is only one factor that will determine the success or otherwise of whatever you are proposing to do: the will power.

Always, tenacity and persistence are the typical characteristics of every successful person.

Try to interview any successful person.

Everyone will agree to state that more than once they have had to stay ahead of any reasonable limit.

They will change their stories, they will change the anecdotes that they tell you, but the substance will remain the same.

To persist means having the courage and the will to pull straight towards your own path, whatever happens and whatever people tell you.

Successful people adapt their actions as they go along, making changes and small changes to the initial strategy until they find the right path.

In short, being "persistent" does not mean being "stupid", but wondering where one has gone wrong and, above all, "learning" from one's mistakes.

At first it is as if we were walking blindfolded in an open space in search of the sea, without having any idea where it is. Initially we have endless possibilities about where to go, most people after a few steps give up research. Those who keep looking can wander for days without encountering a drop of water. Maybe some are just walking around intently, without coming close to the sea and when they realize that, they give up. The others force themselves to learn from that experience to understand when they are going around in circles. Over time (or rather experience), they will learn not to be fooled by puddles and will finally find a riverbed. It is the awareness that the sea exists that sends these people forward. Maybe they will walk that river in the wrong direction, but when they realize it, they will have the strength to go back and finally reach the sea. Only through mistakes can we reach the sea. Only the mistakes allow us to restrict the possibilities of action and, after having committed the sufficient amount of errors, find the right path.

Successful people are therefore neither afraid, nor defeated, nor wrong.

They know that they are part of the game of their growth and they react by clenching their teeth and squeezing their brains. They make it work to get the most information out of their mistakes. This mental process is called resilience.

Resilience comes from the Latin "salio", a word was used by the ancients to indicate who could jump from an upside-down boat. Then he pointed out those who resisted difficulties were able to be saved.

So, when it comes to resilience from a psychological point of view, it simply means the ability to build an opportunity even from adversity.

A proverb says:

"When the wind of change blows, some build walls, other windmills."

Therefore, developing one's resilience is what makes it possible to pursue even very difficult goals, despite the constant presence of obstacles.

In fact, starting a business doesn't always mean being successful, indeed often the first time it fails.

It is thanks to the resilience that emerges from failure that one does not allow oneself to fall into despair, but one draws strength and teaching from one's mistakes.

Maybe right now you are in a difficult time or you are experiencing doubts about your business, so the time has come to develop your resilience.

To develop resilience, the ABCDE technique can be used. It is simply a series of observations to be made whenever there is a difficulty or an error.

This technique is useful for becoming aware of the fact that our behavior and our reactions to negative events do not depend directly on events, but on our evaluation of them.

The sentence I just wrote is one of the cornerstones of personal growth. The human being has an unimaginable power: whatever event happens to him, it is he who chooses what meaning to give it and therefore what reaction to have.

We are so used to reacting mechanically to life events that we have forgotten our extraordinary ability, the essence of resilience.

The ABCDE technique serves to remind us of this ability. Let's look at it in detail. The letters that give the name to this technique are nothing more than the initials:

A for Adversity. The first letter indicates the difficulties we can encounter in our lives, the negative events over which we have no control, and which inevitably happen. They can include small "tragedies" such as a test gone wrong, or much more relevant difficulties.

B for Beliefs. The second letter indicates our beliefs. The set of beliefs that we have developed over the course of our lives represent the filter through which we perceive reality. In fact, our perception of reality is always subjective, as are our reactions.

C for Consequences. The third letter of the model indicates our emotional and physical reactions to events. As you may have understood, these reactions are always the sum of the event and our beliefs.

D for Discussion. The first 3 letters indicate the normal sequence adopted by our mind in front of an event. With the letter D, resilience comes into play. When we are able to question our irrational reactions, we begin to regain control of our lives.

E for Effects. Unlike the reactions (consequences) the effects derive from our questioning of our beliefs. If we often feel that we have no control over our reactions, the effects, as a result of a process of reworking our mind, are fully under our control.

Training our resilience therefore means continually asking ourselves a question in the face of life events: "What is good about what is happening?", or "What is the best meaning that I can attribute to what is happening?"

Initially this exercise may seem like the classic nonsense of "positive thinking", but if properly applied, it will allow you to take the helm of your life back into your hand, bringing out the best from each event and deciding for yourself what your reactions will be.

Then:

Do not run away from situations of hardship, but accept them and try to gain an advantage or a lesson anyway;

Start by overcoming the small obstacles of everyday life. If you let yourself be defeated by a small problem how will you deal with the bigger ones?

Constantly think about the goal you want to achieve and let the desire to succeed be stronger than abandoning everything.

Always question yourself.

"Always think about how you could do better and challenge yourself".
E.Musk

Resilience therefore helps you overcome failures and disappointments, but for those who want to achieve the goal of a successful business, it cannot work without the famous: willpower.

Willpower, unlike resilience, is the one that allows you to achieve a goal thanks to the constancy of your actions.

Those who have will power are able to give up a free weekend to study or work on their project. It is the one that helps them choose to get up every morning at 5, although they are not forced to dedicate themselves to the goals set, etc.

This desire to do, not to give up, to continue undeterred to follow a goal, is what allows you to succeed in life sooner or later to achieve concrete results, fighting the main enemies for every business: laziness, procrastination, and thought not to make it.

How to develop willpower?

Every time we postpone what we should do to do what we want, we are putting present pleasure before our future happiness. It is a choice on which we have full power, and it is a choice that we are called upon to make dozens of times a day.

Becoming aware of this choice is the first step to increase our willpower.

Imagine you are sitting at the restaurant: for your health (you have put on several pounds lately) you have decided to do without the cake, so when the waiter arrives you cannot order it.

But when you're about to ask for coffee, you pass the cart with the sweets and suddenly change your mind.

"A portion of profiteroles, thank you ... Ah, sorry, even that piece of fruit cake remained alone".

... and succumb to temptation, without shame.

Eat and enjoy, and then cry.

When the biochemical gratification is long gone and you feel the stomach swollen like a bagpipe, you regret it. And while you are calculating the calories with your new app, you say that this was the last time, it was time to change your life (starting tomorrow though).

But meanwhile you are there, sunk on the couch, and you wonder what happened, why did the dessert cart get the better of your health dangers?

The answer is simple.

The dessert cart is here in the present, while the risks to your health are there, far away, in the future.

You repeat that ...

"It is not definite that something will happen to me just from a few extra pounds."

The risks are very far, as you can see, impalpable, difficult to see with the naked eye, and moreover they do not have the luminous charm of those chocolate-covered balls that from the cart of sweets enchanting you like the sirens of Ulysses.

What happened in your mind, in front of the sweets, takes the name of devaluation of the future.

To develop the strength of will, it is necessary to become aware of the devaluation of the future and to know which mechanisms regulate the will power, to overturn the situation.

If you go to the gym and you train seriously, your muscles become hypertrophied, swollen, giving you more strength. But if you don't go, over time, they become hypotrophic, and even getting out of a chair becomes a problem.

The same happens to our will, which like a mental muscle, is sensitive to training: it becomes hypertrophic if you train it, and hypotrophic if you don't use it.

A simple example.

You say: "Tomorrow I'm going to run," but the next day you postpone, resorting to more or less refined self-deceptions (too much wind, too hot, too many people...). And the next day you postpone again, and then again, accumulating weeks and months of apathy and reluctance, until you give up completely.

Your legs lose tone and the pounds pile up, but it's not the only damage, it's just the most obvious one.

The most important and dangerous damage is what is produced in your inner world, every time you give in and send back.

Your will weakens, as your legs become hypotrophic, and your self-esteem suffers, sending back to you a disconsolate image of you that brings you down and depresses you.

But it is not over, even your tolerance threshold weakens, pushing you to yield even to the smallest temptations, those to which you once managed to resist.

The effect of this vicious circle, often, is the anxiety that assails you when, now with a hypotrophic will and a very low tolerance threshold, you try to take control of your life in vain.

And failure after failure you come to think of what you should never think of:

"I know I will fail again this time, so why keep trying?"

Where to start from?

Being aware of the deceptions of our mind (e.g. the devaluation of the future) is certainly the first step to respect our intentions and to form good habits.

But if we wish to radically change the course of our lives, we must make a real "mental leap", learning to see habits as the training ground for our will.

Thus, going for a run in the morning, for example, will no longer be a simple way to get back in shape, but the tool to make your will hypertrophic, to raise your tolerance threshold and to strengthen your self-esteem.

Awareness is a necessary condition, but not enough to achieve the desired change.

If you are determined to increase your willpower, you will have to do it every day: I guarantee that it will not be pleasant, but the rewards that await you at the end of this journey far exceed the sacrifices you will have to undergo.

Here are 3 practical exercises to start with to train the muscle of willpower:

1) MIT: most important tasks. MITs are nothing more than the most important activities we should / would like to complete every day. Whether it is physical activity, study or tasks related to an important project that we are following, MITs are those points on our to-do list that, if concluded, give meaning to the whole day. Choose every day from a minimum of 1 to a maximum of 3 MIT and complete them, whatever happens. This simple practice will allow you to take your willpower to a high level. An example of a very effective task that could help you in a particular way is the silence technique. The technique consists of not speaking for a whole day, except in response to direct questions.

Remaining silent for a whole day, you do nothing but condition yourself to do what you consciously decide to do, without limiting yourself to reacting continuously.

The more control you will be able to have over your willpower, the more it will grow.

Don't allow external conditions, chance or others to decide what you can and can't do, what you can and can't get. Always make your own decisions first and respect them using your will power.

2) The 30-day trial. This simple technique, made famous by blogger Steve Pavlina, consists of developing a new habit in 30 days. Choose a new habit and decide to respect it for at least 30 days at any cost. Once the "trial period" is over, you can choose whether to make the new habit part of your life or not. In these 30 days, not only will you create a new habit, but you will increase your self-discipline and willpower every day.

According to a study by Case Western Reserve University, small changes in our daily routines can gradually increase our willpower. Here are some practical examples:

1. In the morning, when you wake up, brush your teeth using your left hand (your right hand if you are left-handed).

2. Replace the first gesture you take every morning (smoking a cigarette, turning on your computer, etc.) with a healthier action.

If you are tempted to check your smartphone, refer to it for a few minutes.

In general, get used to doing what you're not used to doing, just because you decide to do it; just like if you had to write like a left-handed person.

Imposing your willpower on these small actions allows you to start a chain effect that, with every small achievement, follows a more important goal.

3) Steel promises. The last technique I want to talk to you about is the steel promises, which we could summarize with this sentence: you always keep what you promise. Keeping everything we promise, not only increases our willpower, but also has a tremendous impact on our self-esteem and the esteem others have of us.

"Do not be sorry for what you could not do, regret only when you could and did not want."

Mao Tse-tung.

Willpower is a muscle: use it or you will lose it.

The combination of willpower and resilience make you ready to face any challenge.

4 VALUE AND PERSUASION

In addition to the will, I also want to give you some ideas about the concepts of value and persuasion. The goal is not just "knowing how to sell your products or services", but also "knowing how to choose the right partners". If we know how to look beyond the "packaging", we can understand the true value of what is proposed to us and consequently of those who could potentially collaborate with us.

I want to clarify that you can also use the most effective and sophisticated technique of persuasion, but if "inside the package", the product or service is not up to expectations, the customer will not be satisfied. A customer who is not satisfied, is not just a customer who will no longer buy, but a source of bad publicity. Bad publicity totally negates the effect of any persuasion. So "increasing the value" or "persuading to buy" has a positive effect only when you manage to keep the expectations you create. If your product has low value, it is very complex to maintain a high perceived value over time. Persuade, but do it with logic.

Every moment we make hundreds of decisions without realizing that we are doing it. People are surrounded by persuasive messages all day long: from verbal suggestions from friends and colleagues to advertising images along the way, to radio and television commercials, on the internet and other media. To defend ourselves from the high number of stimuli that "bombard us", we have developed the ability to ignore them or pay the least attention to them and, if they affect us minimally, we raise the level of attention. When a person enters an eCommerce platform, he proves to have some sort of commercial intention.

Well, given this propensity to buy... are you showing a message that can turn that interested visitor into a buyer? Perception is not reality, especially when it comes from something apparently objective like the value of a product. In fact, the perceived value of a specific product is rather malleable. There are countless studies and anecdotes that support the idea that it is possible to modify few elements to increase the perception of the value of the product.

First of all, what is meant by perceived value? The value perceived by the customer is expressed by the global evaluation of the usefulness of a product, based on the perception of what is received (GET component) and what is given (GIVE component). Other authors, instead, define value exclusively as a trade-off between perceived quality and perceived price. More generally, the perception of value emerges from the comparison (trade-off) between the benefits received from a specific object or service and the sacrifices (monetary and otherwise) necessary to obtain and benefit from these benefits.

According to Rory Sutherland, one of the biggest gaps in marketing is not being able to identify the overall essence of a product or service, not only based on its value, but also on its meaning. The same product can in fact have a different meaning for different people and, the best thing, would be to propose it for what it objectively represents (even if in reality there are objective costs linked to the realization of a product). There is therefore a great opportunity to influence the perception of the value of a product or service, as well as that of optimizing the customer's experience so as to satisfy needs and desires. Thus, maximizing conversions (people who actually buy).

It is possible to increase the perceived value of the product without actually increasing its objective value (including costs). Such as? Changing people's perception. In our everyday life we can find different examples:

Brand painkillers, in the common imagination, are more effective in reducing pain. In reality all the pills have the same "objective quality" but each individual prefers some over others.

People are convinced that, after washing the car, you drive better.

The tributes push people to make endless queues just to use them. Although the quality and price of the objects is often paltry.

Too many choices decrease sales.

A further study by Tor Wager investigates the behavior of consumers in relation to the evaluation of the value of the product based on the results they expect. The sample of subjects had to evaluate the effectiveness of a drug against headaches. The participants were divided into two groups

(A/B test). The first was given aspirin, while the second was given placebo pills. The results showed that even the second group found a decrease in pain, not only mental but also in terms of physiological reactions. In other words, the mere sight of the packaging of a drug for headache activates the expectation of a reduction in pain, which generates a neural activity aimed at lowering the disease itself. All this to say that, to influence a behavior, it is possible to exploit irrational aspects that are very often considered more than rational elements such as price and quality. In fact, value is not simply evaluated on an economic basis of unity, but on the basis of an evaluation of value-based pricing.

In other words, the price of a product is defined based on what customers would pay to buy it. The value perceived as "pushed" at the actual cost is used. There are different ways to calculate the optimal price, one of these is of course the A/B Test. Advertising and public relations are other effective activities to increase perceived value.

Therefore, it is possible to understand how the context and the global vision can modify the perception of a situation. For this reason, the reformulation of a price is an excellent solution to change the perceived value of a product. The following is an example of a car manufacturer that has effectively modulated perceived costs without affecting the quality of the product. Copywriting is an absolutely central aspect for the re-contextualization of an offer.

The scarcity effect was conceptualized by Cialdini in 1987 during the realization of the studies he did on the social influence, and even though it is a fairly well-known theme, it is always attractive, so much so that it continues to produce benefits in advertising. Cialdini suggested that the "scarcity", or the limited availability of a product, produces a greater desire to try to get what is scarce. It seems that people immediately establish a mental equation: the rarer a product the more value it has. This implicit process is a quick choice of thinking that simplifies decision-making by reducing cognitive effort. In other words, many times our mind does not have all the data or does not consider them to accurately value the real price of the product, so when we find a desirable product the mental representation is activated: rare = of value, and immediately decides to buy. The desire! People like to own what others cannot have! But the power of scarcity goes far beyond this: an incredible experiment conducted some tens of years ago in the United States shows how we are all unconsciously influenced by the apparent scarcity, even if it is simply an impression of ours.

In 1975, research conducted by some American professors (Worchel, Lee and Adewole) required a series of people to evaluate chocolate biscuits. Ten cookies were placed in one jar and two cookies of the same type in another container. The latter received a higher rating than the larger ones, although they were exactly the same. That's not all: the larger jar cookies tasted at the beginning, when they were more numerous, received a lower rating than the biscuits tasted when they were less. Marketers often use strategies based on scarcity, with phrases like "Limited Offer", "Last Items Left" or "While stocks last"! The idea that poorly available products are more appealing is not new. The new iPhone MUST be excellent if hundreds of people queue up to grab one of the few available, right? In eCommerce, a variety of tactics are used to create scarcity, such as showing how many units of that product remain in stock.

The eCommerce sites have the advantage of providing immediate and credible feedback to visitors about the level of units in stock and are the ideal environment to experiment with the so-called scarcity effect. Traditionally, the scarcity effect uses two variables: "limited quantities" (last pieces in stock exhaustion) and "count-down" (product available up to a certain date/time). However, these two approaches are not characteristic only of the eCommerce platform, in fact it is possible to use them also in paper brochures or speaking in person with the customer. Let's see, specifically, how it is possible to use the dynamics of the web to increase the effectiveness of the scarcity effect. For example, Amazon, which has some experience on the marketing techniques applied to eCommerce, does not limit itself to alerting consumers to the "limited quantity" but, for the last pieces, allows free shipping. Time combined with the opportunity to save is an effective mix to stimulate impulse buying. It is also possible to show the scarcity of an object variable (such as size or color) by ticking the one that is not available or by coloring the font in a different color. Also highlighting how many people are looking at the card of that product at a given time helps to create the urgency of the purchase for fear that the available quantities will end. Booking.com, as can be seen from the image below, effectively uses this approach.

It is also possible to use a voucher with a time limit and include a countdown timer that warns of the expiry of the discount voucher. The "flash sales" are another widespread tactic to create the urgency of the purchase that relies on scarcity. If you do not buy now you will pay more, or you can never buy again, or you will not be happy. It is super effective for the conversion of buyers who are strongly attracted to the goods on sale.

Another exploitable heuristic at eCommerce level is the "hyperbolic discount" connected to the tendency of individuals to systematically overestimate immediate costs and benefits (and to underestimate future ones). This implies the adoption of short-sighted behaviors, in the sense of a lack of awareness of the consequences of one's lifestyle in relation to the sustainability of one's financial endowment. According to this principle, most people prefer a €20 discount immediately (therefore close) to a €50 discount in 6 months (higher discount but farther away). Another example is when you choose to pay for an item purchased with an advance and pay for it after months. With this approach the tangible cost is reduced (the one that must be paid immediately) the amount that remains to be paid (less tangible) is "mentally discounted" by the buyer due to the "distance of payment in the future".

Overstock.com instead chooses an even more direct approach: replacing "quantities are limited" with a more alarming "Sell out Risk high!". And, even more evident, it does not remove out of stock products but leaves them in the window (and Google continues to index them), marking them with a clearly visible "Sold Out".

At first glance it may seem like a risky move. Showing a customer an unavailable product could arouse his interest and push him to look for it elsewhere. However, these "Sold Out" products strongly consolidate the credibility of the limited quantity alerts related to other products and add a sense of urgency to the shopping process. Credibility is an important factor and realizing precise communicative messages reinforces the concept. "Last two pieces available" is more effective than "limited quantity" and, even better, it would provide a dynamic display of inventory changes.

Man is naturally inclined to help a fellow man in a disinterested way if he feels empathy for him. Toi and Batson (1982) asked students to listen to the recording of one of their classmates who described the dynamics of a serious car accident that caused both her legs to break, making it very difficult to follow and stay on par with university lectures. The expected experimental conditions were:

1. High empathy: subjects are asked, as they listen, to imagine how their partner feels and to imagine the change in her life.

2. Low empathy: request for objectivity, without concern for the girl's feelings.

3. High social cost: students will see their partner in a wheelchair every day.

4. Low social cost: the girl will always study at home and the subjects will never see her.

Therefore, the sample is asked to read a letter from the girl asking for help regarding the revision of the introductory notes of the psychology course. The results of the study show that in case of high empathy, the subjects do not think about the cost (in terms of negative feeling of always being in front of the person they did not help) that they could pay in case of no help, with equivalent acceptance percentages (around 80%), while in the case of low empathy it does not reach 40%. From this experiment it emerges that the creation of situations of high empathy develops on a sense of disinterested altruism. A reality that applies this concept well is Crate and Barrel, which invests part of the advertising budget in charitable contributions to DonorsChoose. Donations, as well as for institutions, are key aspects also for consumers who, knowing they are "doing good", are more likely to make purchases. The recent survey "Altruism is powerful differentiator for luxury brands" pointed out that the sale of products involving donations is more appreciated:

94% of consumers reports that they would pass to a competing brand if it supported a beneficial cause.

20% of the sample is willing to buy a more expensive product if part of the proceeds is given to charity.

Every purchase and transaction hides behind itself a certain degree of risk perceived by the customer. The perception of risk is measured mainly at the level of the possible economic loss: if I buy the good "x" and does not work according to my expectations, the money spent is lost. Even if the perception of money loss is in many cases the first element related to the perception of risk, there are ramifications with much more important implications and not limited to the simple danger of an economic loss. Let's look at them in detail below:

In its many facets, emotional risk is present in numerous purchases both in the B2B and B2C fields. This particular condition can be linked to the opinion and possible blame that other people (colleagues, superiors, friends, clients, relatives) can address to the person who is responsible for a particular purchase choice. In some cases, the emotional factor may be the main element that influences the buying behavior. This can easily happen in many professions that establish a helping relationship with the client (psychologists, doctors, etc.) and also in some sectors of professional counseling.

Complex purchasing decisions can put the entire security and the future of a company at risk. The choice of particular suppliers, technologies and/or machinery or the acquisition of new and innovative methods and processes are only examples of elements that can be sources of real risk and perceived by those who have to make important decisions. Anyone who is seriously determined to discover decision-making levers, and go deeper into the internal customer choice mechanisms, cannot ignore this risk analysis. It is important to note that the classic tools for investigating customer behavior and feedback rarely allow access to this type of knowledge with the details and honesty necessary to undertake effective marketing and communication actions.

Any experience takes place in phases. Even a purchase. Credibility and trust are built in the first contact phases (within the first 3 seconds of interaction) - primacy effect - and are consolidated in the exit phases and in the last things we see or final interactions - recency effect. This does not only concern lived experiences, but also the reading of messages or interpersonal relationships. In these relationships, the greeting and farewell phases are fundamental. The warmth or coldness of such moments has a decisive effect. A specific persuasive problem concerns the order of presentation most effective in presenting the topics. The effects analyzed by the Yale school are in particular those of primacy (tendency to remember the first elements of a list) and recency (tendency to remember the last elements of a list), which are both active: in other words, the subjects tend to remember the initial arguments and the endings of a persuasive speech. Specifically, the primacy effect is reflected above all in the long term because the incoming information has more time to settle. The recency effect supports when an action is to be performed "immediately after", because the information is still in the short-term memory. This makes it necessary to conceive the structure of a message so as to have more effective arguments at the beginning and at the end of the message.

In addition to the pitfall of mistrust, we come up against another factor that is becoming increasingly important and decisive in the purchase: the user experience. One of the factors that most affects the success of an eCommerce depends on how it is presented. Even online, the first impression greatly influences all the others, so it is important to create first of all a pleasant, linear and attractive homepage that best transmits trust, quality and clarity. The navigation must favor the discovery of the different categories and sub-categories in an intuitive way (for example women-accessories-bags).

Persuasion is not the result of a single optimized message, nor of a single offer that attracts visitors. All this to convince the visitor to take the next step, and to complete the action we want to take (the purchase, of course!).

"Not brute force, but persuasion and faith are the real queens of this world."

Thomas Carlyle.

Persuasion is a fundamental tool that you should always have on hand in your toolbox.

You may have studied months for your exam and memorized every page of the book, but at the same time, failing to convince the professor about your actual preparation.

You can have in mind the most brilliant idea of this planet for your work, yet not being able to present it correctly to your colleagues or your bosses (or in our case, as we shall see, to your investors).

You can have a product or service that can truly revolutionize the life of your customers, and at the same time not be able to sell it because you are not able to transmit the real value.

In all these cases, learning effective persuasion techniques can be useful for achieving the results you deserve.

A study conducted by Professor Stiff, reported in the book "Persuasive Communication", showed that asking the simple question "Why not?" Has a high success rate in turning a dry no into a more accommodating "Yes".

The objective of the "Why not?" Technique is indeed to transform a definitive answer ("No") into a simple obstacle to be overcome. Putting the question "Why not?" Forces the interlocutor to have to provide objections, more or less logical, that we can manage much more simply than direct rejection.

Furthermore, the more the objections are weak, the more we come to create a cognitive dissonance in the mind of our interlocutor, who in the desperate search for coherence will end up meeting us. In short: if there is no valid reason for not doing something, why not do it?!

Directly from the experience of door-to-door salesmen, door technology is born ... in the face! When we want to get a certain result from our interlocutor, we should make a request that we ourselves consider too high and not very reasonable: this request will undoubtedly be followed by a metaphorical door in the face, or a refusal; at this point we should immediately follow the real request we had in mind: compared with the first one in fact, the new request will appear more modest and reasonable.

This technique bases its effectiveness on the natural tendency of our mind to make comparisons. If we provide the right term of comparison, no request will appear excessive.

Don't you feel like asking your boss for a disproportionate pay rise?! Then use the "face to face" technique on yourself when defining a goal:

"Aim for the moon, no matter what goes you will find yourself among the stars."

The third persuasion technique that we are talking about and that is always inspired by our "funny" door-to-door salesmen, is the "foot in the door" technique. Unlike the technique of "face to face", the goal of this third technique is to make a request so trivial and obvious to be able to snatch a first, but very important "yes" to our interlocutor.

I am sure that you have seen this technique applied dozens of times: have you ever met the guys who ask you if you've ever read a book?! Or to answer yet another call from a call center operator who asks you if you use the phone?! The goal of these idiotic questions is precisely to snatch a "yes": it is shown that people who accept a first small request tend to accept even more demanding subsequent requests.

In my experience I have seen this technique often badly used and abused: but do you want to put the fun of neutralizing these babies with their own weapons?! Next time they ask you if you have ever read a book, ask them if they have ever seen a movie!

Sometimes to convince someone all we have to provide is a motivation. As our motivation may seem weak or trivial, providing it greatly increases our chances of success.

An example? In a 1978 study by Langer, the freshmen enrolled by the Professor had to ask a simple question to their colleagues (unaware) in the copy shop; here is the question used: "I need to use the photocopier before you, because I have to make photocopies". Although the reason given was weak, surprisingly the students who used this question obtained a "yes" in 90% of the cases.

The main verbal communication strategies used in persuasion are:

1. To order, that is, using a language that encourages the other to make experiences that can change his opinion, his point of view.

It is not a matter of impositions or orders in the strict sense, but of a suggestive and persuasive communication, which evokes in people the feeling of being able to do something completely different from what they are used to, overcoming their own limits.

An example is Gandhi's maxim "be the change you want to see in the world", which imposes nothing on the listener, but urges him to new actions and to improve himself.

2. To evoke, that is, to use a language that, through analogies and images, helps to project oneself into concrete situations.

There is no need to think of anything too complex: even the very simple phrase "I slept like a child" fulfills this technique of Strategic Dialogue, with an image that evokes a clear experience in the listener. Another example is the phrase of Fernando Pessoa: "I carry all the wounds of the battles I have avoided", thanks to which an abstract concept such as giving up evokes the concrete contours of wounds that damage ourselves first.

Evoking allows a specific message to be transmitted without information exchange, persuading others to act in a certain way.

3. To restructure, that is, change the structure and sequence of words used by a person to offer them different points of view without changing the content of his speech, in an indirect way.

To restructure you can use paraphrases, strategic questions that guide the interlocutor in a certain direction, narratives, suggestive aphorisms.

For example, Oscar Wilde's aphorism could be used to restructure the overprotective behavior of two parents: "with the best intentions the worst effects are produced". Immediately the two parents would have a different perception of their attitude, and this would lead them to change spontaneously.

Persuasion also uses clear non-verbal communication strategies:

Musicality of words and modulation of the voice: for the purpose of persuasion, the emotions elicited by a message are as important as the content. For this reason, the use of a musical and harmonic language is fundamental, which makes wide use of assonances and dissonances.

For example, the phrase "everyone creates what causes him pain" which, through the assonance of sounds, invites reflection on the content of the message.

Depending on the feeling to be evoked, some sounds should be preferred over others, as well as modulating the pauses, tone and volume of the voice, so as to fascinate the listener. Moreover, the modulation of the voice makes communication more alive: think of the conferences in which the speakers always use the same tone, rhythm and volume of voice, quickly losing the attention of the public. This is precisely what should be avoided if we want to persuade others and get in tune with them.

Look and mimic: according to some studies, to make a good first impression on others we have about 30 seconds, just the time needed to say goodbye, say our name and little else (and of these 30 seconds, as we have seen, the most important are the first 3).

Therefore, gaze and mimicry are necessary to evoke the right sensations: maintaining eye contact helps to establish empathy and arouse sympathy, while looking at someone too insistently could make them uncomfortable and break the tune.

The same is true for facial expressions: a forced and unnatural mimicry arouses mistrust, but a relaxed smile conveys a sense of welcome and understanding.

Posture and movements: one of the most effective strategies to establish a connection with others is to reflect their postures and their movements, always in a natural way.

For example, tilting the head on the same side of our interlocutor or crossing the legs in the same direction, unconsciously, helps us to establish a relationship, regardless of the content of the speech.

Even the distance can increase the harmony but be careful: if we are too close, we risk creating discomfort, if we are too far away, we will transmit a feeling of detachment. It is up to us to understand, from time to time, the right measure.

According to Harvard professor Gerald Zaltman, 95% of users' purchasing decisions are made in the subconscious.

Decision making is complicated for the human mind. For this, as we have already mentioned before, the fewer options are offered to the user, the more likely he will have to choose between one of them.

This is one of the persuasion techniques that also apply to the communication process.

Barry Schwartz popularized the theory of choice paralysis in a TED intervention in which he helped some marketing managers learn how to sell. And make consumers choose. If there are many options, consumers become paralyzed.

Imagine you are in a store looking for a salad dressing. You get to the shelf and find 250 options. Choosing between them will take you more than you imagined. Instead, if you find only two choices, making the right decision will take you less time.

And above all, even if it does not seem, this decision will make you happier, since your subconscious will not torment you thinking that you should have chosen something else.

One of the main mistakes in digital marketing (I will never tire of repeating it) is to think that the more options exist, the better. When it comes to optimizing your content to convert, this idea is counterproductive. Remember, too many options reduce the chances of conversion. I repeat and repeat many times, because many entrepreneurs make this mistake without being able to avoid it.

Even if you think you have to be politically correct in all your communications, strong language is one of the most powerful persuasion techniques that exist. And you will understand it through a real example:

One study divided 88 users into three groups to see which of the three discourses was more effective or caused more impact. Obviously, the only difference between the speeches was that one of them contained the word "cursed" at the beginning of the sentence.

When the attitudes of the participants were verified, those who had been exposed to speeches that included this slight obscenity, seemed more inclined to buy. That is, the word "cursed" increased the perception of the audience by the intensity it brought. Or, in other words, he could persuade the recipients of the communication. And, moreover, the credibility regarding the product was not compromised.

Strong language succeeds in attracting people's attention and helps to persuade. So, one of the persuasion techniques you need to put into practice is the intensity of your communications.

Steve Jobs, despite his correct and emotional presentation style, used the word "crazy" in various speeches. This term communicated intensity. He was passionate about his products and managed to convey this intensity to his audience. Consumers like their salesman to feel this passion

Have you ever thought that if a user abandons you, you don't care? It may seem counter-productive but it makes sense.

To get a loyal community, you need to be able to tell users that if they are not 100% on your side, they can leave. So, if you want to sell a product you have to launch it towards a correct target. And with a step like that you are already discarding a good part of users.

Mystery has always been one of the most powerful and used persuasion techniques. Most people move, on many occasions, towards the mystery.

So, you can use this persuasive weapon in your favor. If you create curiosity, emotion or noise, you will capture the attention of users.

Most people want to do right actions. Surveys show that giving people who have more needs makes people happier. So, what would happen if you yourself helped someone?

It is precisely the value proposition of Toms. With the idea that buying a pair of shoes, another pair will be donated to needy people, the brand makes sure that users feel good and conversions increase accordingly.

Do you know what this technique of persuasion refers to? Fear of losing an opportunity. As this article in The New York Times points out, "we feel the pain of losing more intensely than the pleasure of winning". In other words, everyone likes to win but someone hates losing.

For this reason, in terms of communication, you should take advantage of this technique to show the user that he is about to miss an opportunity. In general, when you sell a product, you try to make it clear to the user what profit you get by purchasing it. Its benefits. Obviously, the drawbacks of the purchase are not underlined.

It's a matter of changing the tone: spend less space talking about the benefits and invest more in explaining what the user might miss if they don't buy the product or service.

5 STARTUP DEFINITION

Next, we find the second section: it contains many valuable practical tips.

According to Steve Blank, a startup is "a temporary organization looking for a replicable and scalable business model".

To propose a second definition of startup, according to Eric Ries a startup is a human institution designed to offer new products or services in conditions of extreme uncertainty.

A third definition to understand what a start-up is, is offered by Paul Graham, who says that a startup is a company designed to grow quickly.

There are four characteristics necessary to be in the presence of a real startup: scalability, replicability of the business model, intrinsic innovation (of process or product) and temporariness.

Repeatability means that a startup's business model can be repeated in different geographical areas and in different time periods without requiring major changes.

Ask yourself the following question: is the business model I am structuring allowing me to have a continuity of application that is independent of the context, market conditions and the volatility of fashions?

Scalability is the ability of a startup to grow exponentially using few resources.

Ask yourself the following question: Is the business model I am structuring allowing me to expand, without encountering limits linked to scarcity of resources? Can I move from 1 customer to 1,000,000 customers within a few days? Can I reach millions and millions of people very quickly? We will see the scalability later in more depth.

Innovation (process or product) is a necessary condition when it comes to startups. Startups are born to satisfy a need that is not yet satisfied (or to create a need that is not yet evident). They are born to subvert the "status quo". They are born to upset (or create) a market.

That is, they are born to innovate.

Ask yourself the following question: do I have an innovation that brings a substantial advantage (10x or more) compared to what currently exists?

The definition of "startup" is temporary. The defined phase of "startup" is in fact transitory and represents the first phase of the company growth path that will lead it (hopefully) to become a big company.

Without these features, we can hardly say that we are in front of a startup.

But then can the new pizza shop under the house be called startup? Absolutely not... unless you invent a new franchise model that allows you to open stores in an unlimited number of countries, quickly and gaining very, very high market shares.

What to do if your final idea does not match the definition of startup? No problem, most concepts that will follow are also valid for traditional companies.

In summary, the startup is defined as a temporary and unstructured organization, looking for a replicable and scalable business model. Basically, born from the desire to resolve a problem, it needs to find a business model that allows it to grow, grow, grow and still grow...

6 VALIDATION PROCESS

I have an idea and I have the experience to control it. This is the embryonic phase, in which the idea begins to take the contours of an organized project.

I have to understand if my idea can work, if I really solve a need and if there is a potential market somewhere in the world (my experience should help me in any case). I have to do it quickly, spending little (remember that our maximum ceiling is $100) and working effectively.

No one (or almost) is willing to finance a project in this embryonic state. Friends, family and fools are the only ones willing to do it... and I dare say that it is very good.

We must validate the market, not create a finished product. We must understand whether to go ahead or to let it go. We need to understand if our idea can turn into a product or service and if people are willing to pay for this product or service.

It is a very delicate phase that the startupper, madly in love with his idea, should conduct in a strictly "objective" manner (it is very difficult, I know).

If there is no market and there are no people willing to pay for what I would like to offer, then it is better to "switch off" (or evaluate a change of strategy before letting go of the grip) by concentrating one's resources (physical, psychological, economic) to another project. You know what you want to do with your life, it's just a matter of changing your perspective, without losing sight of our goal.

In this phase the first funding is received only if the entrepreneur is able to convince thanks to his experience and the level of innovation of the idea he has in mind.

Here the concept of MVP is introduced, an acronym that stands for Minimum Viable Product. It is called, in a nutshell, the wording that defines a pre-launch phase in which the startupper tests the validity of its idea, putting it on display and testing the public's taste. An MVP is basically a first version of the product that you want to launch, containing only the main functions of it (or almost always none, such as the Dropbox MVP which consisted simply in a video). This basic version is distributed to the public for the sole purpose of collecting opinions from consumers. In practice, an idea is distributed, not a product. In this phase, only the opinions of consumers are needed: the more you invest in giving shape to your idea at this stage, the more you risk throwing time, money and energy; do the bare minimum to be understandable. A study phase that provides specific indications, on which to then be able to calibrate one's own activity.

Regardless of the method you use to validate your idea, you should always keep in mind the concept of product market fit.

Product Market Fit indicates the extent to which a product/service is able to meet the needs of a specific market.

Be careful though. It is not enough to know that you have the right product/service for the right market, so that sales can take off: reaching the PMF also means knowing how to conquer that market, transforming potential customers into paying customers.

So, your startup reaches the Product Market Fit when the product/service offered meets the needs of a certain target group and you know how to sell that product/service to them.

Why is PMF so important for your startup? You have probably already understood this: reaching the PMF means having the proof that you are selling the right product/service to the right customers.

If you're not selling, then you don't have a business. And if you don't have a business, your startup is bound to fail. I am sorry to be so dramatic, but it is the pure truth.

A quick way to understand if your startup has reached the PMF is the famous 40% rule, devised by Sean Ellis.

In essence it is a question of conducting a survey and asking your customers how they would feel if, suddenly, they could no longer have access to a certain product or service. If at least 40% of the interviewed customers says they would feel very disappointed, then congratulations: you have reached Product Market Fit.

The PMF calculated in this way obviously represents only a point of reference and, as such, it must be taken with the right distance anyway: knowing that more than 40% of customers considers your product/service a "must have" does not offer any guarantee for the success of your startup.

To measure the PMF more accurately, it is essential to establish upstream objectives and monitor progress through specific metrics. As an example, here are some metrics that can be very useful for quantifying PMF:

Net Promoter Score (NPS) - is an indicator that measures the probability that your users recommend your product/service to a friend;

Engagement - is a metric that shows the level of user interaction with your product in a given time interval;

Paying users - if your users are willing to pay to buy your product/service, then you are really solving a market problem and, therefore, the PMF is almost a certainty;

Organic user base - how many users can you acquire thanks to word of mouth, without investing in marketing and advertising? The greater the number of these users, the more organic growth will be;

Customer Lifetime Value - is an indicator that measures the prospective value of an individual customer with reference to the foreseeable duration of the relationship with the company;

Churn Rate - indicates the percentage of customers your startup has lost in a certain period of time;

Bounce Rate, Time On Site, Pages For Visit, Returning Visitors - these metrics are very useful if you have an online business or an e-commerce, because they allow you to test users' interest in your products/services.

Reaching the PMF is not as easy and banal as it might seem and, when this does not happen, it is essential to try to identify the causes.

Many startuppers, after having a super-revolutionary brilliant idea, rush headlong into the enterprise and immediately realize the product/service he has in mind, without having the faintest idea of who his customers are. And then he complains that nobody buys it!

You see, one of the worst mistakes that a new entrepreneur can make is starting from the solution to get to the problem, that is to create a product/service and then find the customers who will be willing to buy it: 42% of the startups fails precisely because of this approach mistaken.

If your product/service does not meet the needs and requirements of a specific customer target, then from the market point of view it is useless. The only way to avoid this unpleasant situation is to know your customers first, so then to fit your product to their needs: starting from the product and reaching the Product Market Fit will be almost impossible.

Focusing on the customer and his needs does not mean, however, forgetting the product/service: it is through this that your startup will have to satisfy them.

The problem? If your competitors already sell a higher quality product/service and/or at a lower price, you're screwed: sales will never take off.

In these cases, you have two alternatives:

a) develop a better product/service than those already sold by the competition;

b) target another market.

It is not enough to have a product/service and know who to sell it to, but - more importantly - you also need to know how to sell it.

If you don't know how to attract customers (marketing), how to convert them (sales) and how to get your product/service (distribution) into their hands, then you have a big problem: you miss the link in the chain that connects your product with your customers (but you have already gained experience in this field in your evolutionary path and you know how to control all these aspects).

Ok, you've reached the PMF and the sales are taking off, so the success for your startup is guaranteed, isn't it?

See, Product Market Fit isn't something you reach once and then you don't have to worry about it. The PMF could "vanish" at any time: think of those who were once big in their sector (e.g. Kodak, Nokia, Blockbuster, etc.) and you will realize it.

Why can PMF fail? The reasons are more or less the same as we saw earlier:

you don't know (anymore) who your customers are. The market, whether you know, is changeable: the needs of your customers could change from one day to the next and your product/service could become superfluous sooner than you think; your product/service is not the best. Your competitors will not stand idly by looking at you while your startup conquers the market: they will stay with you, always trying to offer your customers something better;

you don't know (anymore) how to sell your product/service. The marketing and sales strategies and the distribution channels you use today to sell your product/service could quickly become obsolete, sooner than you think, and your competitors will take advantage of it to steal customers.

Product Market Fit and traction are two closely related elements, but they should not be confused.

As I wrote at the beginning, in fact, the PMF is closely linked to the phase where the startup must identify the early adopters, test their real interest and receive feedback. Reaching the PMF means having the right product for the right market and knowing how to sell it, but this does not mean having traction.

Traction is nothing but the validation of your product, that is the proof that someone wants to buy your product: if you have traction, then your startup is offering a product/service that the market wants. And if your product is free (think social media for example), then the traction is a growing user base.

Traction can be represented through an exponential curve: at the beginning it grows very slowly, but then begins to rear up and grow at a high rate in ever shorter time intervals. This is the point where growth literally explodes, accelerating suddenly. Depending on the case, this explosive growth can affect your sales, your profits, the number of customers acquired or even the number of downloads of your mobile app.

Measuring the traction of your startup is easier said than done, since it is necessary to take into account not only the sector, but also a whole series of external and unpredictable market factors.

So how do you tell if your startup has a good traction?

The first step is to try to visualize the future of the organization, identifying clear and specific objectives: clarity of objectives will allow you to understand (and show potential investors) how your startup can grow in relation to market factors and to competition.

Of course, setting goals is not enough. To measure the traction, it is essential to identify the metrics that will be used to define the success of your business: in some cases, the turnover and the number of customers acquired could be excellent indicators of traction, in others they could be misleading.

Let's take an e-commerce company for example... Can Amazon be okay?

For many years the company did not have a significant profitability, mainly due to the high operating costs, but on the other hand its turnover, between 2006 and 2007, started to grow exponentially, reaching 232 billion dollars in 2018.

It is not only the turnover, but also the number of customers, the quantity of products sold, the number of visitors to the site and the average sales margin that have grown. In short, it cannot be said that Amazon has no traction!

Many startups don't fail because they don't have a product, but because they don't have traction. As many Silicon Valley entrepreneurs know, the key to your startup's success does not lie in the originality of what you offer, in the talent of your team or in the amount of funds you can raise from investors.

What really makes the difference between a failed startup and a successful startup is its ability to grow and acquire new customers.

Traction, however, is fundamental not only for the founders and employees, but also for investors: the greater the traction, the easier it will be to attract investors and funds to finance your startup.

Be careful, though: don't forget that investors are still interested in an economic return. This means that if a good traction can attract them, the absence of a business model able to guarantee the profitability of the startup will make it difficult to continue to enjoy their trust and access other funds.

This is why it is fundamental to find patient investors enough to tolerate short-term losses in favor of a long-term return: it is the case of Amazon, which has always had a good traction, but only in recent years has it begun to distribute attractive dividends to the own shareholders.

The PMF, therefore, is a marketing metric, while the traction is a sales metric.

To make it simple, reaching the PMF does not imply also getting the traction. Ok, you know that your product/service pleases the market and you also know how to sell it, but as long as you haven't sold it to a certain number of customers, how do you get proof that your product/service really likes it?

Traction is the proof that the market really wants to buy what you offer. And when you reach the traction, you're no longer just selling to a handful of early adopters: this is the "momentum" in which the virtuous word-of-mouth circle is triggered, and sales start to grow exponentially. On the other hand, none of this is possible without the PMF: if you do not reach the Product Market Fit before, the traction is practically unreachable.

One way to validate your idea with respect to the market is the smoke test.

The smoke test is a test used by computer programmers to evaluate the effectiveness of the basic functions of a software.

In our case the smoke test takes on the same meaning: if you think you have an interesting idea, it is better to test it by acknowledging the behavior of the market and deciding only later whether to implement it, pivot or abound the idea itself. In short: evaluate the effectiveness of your idea before attacking the market with your product or service.

The goal of the smoke test is to find out if the lead is really interested in what you have to offer and you do it by making it believe that your product/service is already available on the market.

A little petty trick? Absolutely not! Indeed, it is the best way to validate your idea and to engage future customers.

If your business idea is to sell organic jams with miraculous properties online, why not prepare the website even before starting production?

If anyone is interested, be sincere, apologize saying that the "jams" are not yet available (but they will be available soon) and that you "used" that click to evaluate the interest on the product. Maybe, in that case, promise customers that you will send some free jar considering the availability (letting you leave an email address to contact them a little later)... and voila... you are validating your idea and you already have people willing to pay even before having launched the product.

The smoke test therefore brings with it a series of interesting advantages, including:

Demonstrated interest (with which you can then entice investors);

Possibility of learning and optimization (by launching more smoke tests simultaneously, for example);

Possibility to organize the production starting from the request (if you have a product startup do not underestimate this aspect);

Customer loyalty (you have the email of those who pressed the button. You were sincere and honest. The purpose was not to deceive, but to get better feedback).

The example we have given above is a trivial example, but I hope useful, to understand the potential of the smoke test.

Another method of validation is that of interviews.

Validating is receiving feedback.

Validating is applying the good old "scientific method" in which, acting to refute hypotheses, we arrive at the logical conclusion.

Starting from the product or service is simply too risky. Starting from the problem, wearing the clothes of the customers, is the right approach.

To put it to the Steve Blank: "Get Out of the Building" that we can translate into: as soon as the basic hypotheses are clear, leave your office and go talk to potential customers to see if the problem you want to solve is really felt and to understand if the solution you propose is really the right one.

But how should interviews be managed? Who should you interview? What method should you follow?

Interviewing the friend, the relative, the cousin is not the right solution. Their opinion would be less objective (exactly like yours). They don't want to disappoint you and maybe they're not even afflicted by the problem you're trying to solve. Don't waste time, you wouldn't do anything with that feedback.

In the first instance it is necessary to target customers and identify early adopters.

Identifying the first potential customers will allow you to investigate the problem (or problems) you are trying to solve, modeling the solution based on the feedback received, thus avoiding proceeding "blindly". It will also allow you to "hook" the first paying people for your product or service. Not bad, right?

Who are the early adopters? I like to think that those people are desperate and oppressed by the problem you are trying to solve. They are those people who try to solve it but cannot find a satisfactory solution. In short: those that would do anything to shake off that problem.

Targeting your customers means addressing their validation and interviews by defining specific types of customers. An example would be: single men and women, aged between 30 and 45 and with an annual income of X.

Hands up who has never had an interview that looked like an interrogation. Here, better to avoid.

Conduct the interview in an informal way, leaving the interlocutor in his comfort zone, avoiding the police/guilty effect. Why not in front of a coffee for example? Maybe letting the interviewee choose the most convenient location based on his travels, tastes or availability.

Starting off on the right foot is essential.

Better a few interviews (to the right people, asking the right questions) or collecting 350 surveys in a few days?

In this phase the quality is better than the quantity. Keep quality high by preferring interviews rather than questionnaires. The goal is not the scalability of the information gathered, but its quality.

The interview should follow a logical scheme to refute or validate the hypotheses behind your idea (first of all the problem that you think can affect the interviewees).

The goal is not to ask people if they like the solution you have in mind but try to understand if you have taken the right path. You will never have to talk about your idea, nor will you have to try to sell the pre-packaged solution you've thought of.

Listening is the key word to apply at this stage.

Another fundamental aspect: try to identify the problem/solution binomial without asking directly. Often people cannot focus on a problem so clearly that they can talk about it, let alone a possible solution (which often does not even exist yet). On this aspect it is worthwhile to think about a famous phrase attributed to Ford: "If I had asked my customers what they wanted, their answer would have been: faster horses".

Ask open questions that can put the interviewees at ease and guarantee maximum freedom of expression, so as to capture any suggestions and useful ideas and focus not only on the answer but also on the attitude of the interviewee.

Remember to write down everything the interviewee says, not what you think it means.

Another little tip? Avoid asking questions about the future. Questions like: how much would you pay for a solution that could solve problem X? If there was a product that...? The hypotheses, the projections and all future "ifs" are banned. Setting the interview in this way would run the risk of shifting the focus to the solution (and its validation) and not to the customer/problem binomial. In addition, the future "blurs" the lucidity of people (how easy it is to say: if there was a product that solved this problem, I would definitely use it... I would be willing to pay X... etc.).

The duration of the interview is another fundamental aspect to consider, both in the preparation phase of the interviews and in the execution phase (preparing 150 open questions or wandering talking for 20 minutes of sport risks taking you off the track with respect to the goal).

The interview should be such as to guarantee the desired result without falling into a useless chat.

Expect a duration of between 15 and 25/30 minutes and try to respect the set objective.

Phone interviews save time but hide pitfalls: is the respondent paying close attention to your questions? Do gestures and expressions contradict the answers? Does the interviewee appear bored or not very interested? Therefore, prefer interviews conducted in person, keeping the other options good only if you can't do without them.

Verbal communication is only one of the useful pieces of data to derive from the interview. Be sure to observe the person's body language, transcribing any cues arising from the context or non-verbal communication.

It is usually better to interview one person at a time, avoiding groups of people interviewed simultaneously. We must avoid getting "false" feedback from non-controllable group dynamics (anxiety, mutual influence between people, etc.).

This is true unless our product/service does not respond to problems specifically related to groups of people. In this case, interviewing a person at a time would benefit from his own point of view, which would not allow you to listen to everyone's voice, pondering different opinions and evaluating the dynamics that in the first case it is better to avoid.

Possible Problem/Idea (in order to explain you better what I mean):

You're at the restaurant with friends. A table neighbor has converted to "veganism" and is complaining that the restaurant is not suitable for her food choices.

You wonder why he didn't use an app to find a vegan-friendly restaurant. Let's say we have gone back a few years, there are no such apps yet.

Why not investigate this idea?

How could we structure a useful interview that leads us to validate the problem and the potential client? We set 4 basic questions, from which to start to explore the problem (and the possible client) and to understand if it is worthwhile to deepen the idea.

1. Which is the most complex aspect that, as a vegan, you encounter when eating away from home?

If formulated correctly, the first question will give you very interesting insights on the problem you have hypothesized. Don't anticipate the interviewee but let him talk to you. Such as?

Avoid questions like: "Why is it so hard to find a vegan restaurant in the city?"

Also avoid too general questions, such as: "Is it difficult to be vegan today?"

And if the problem you hypothesized was not obvious, maybe the interviewee will provide you with other problems to explore...

2. How often do you find restaurants, bars, shops that are not suitable for vegans?

Here is a useful indicator. If the answer, from more people, is: "it is the first time that happens to me in many years", perhaps it is worth letting it go.

3. What did you do to solve this problem?

From this question you will get useful insights on possible competitors or on solutions that can be improved and from which to take inspiration. Ask the question concretely and take note of the interviewee's experience.

Avoid questions like: "What would you do to solve this problem".

As we said at the beginning the interviewee might not even know how to answer this question.

4. What didn't you like about the solutions you adopted?

Here is where we can differentiate and create value. Maybe an app already exists, but you can't search for restaurants based on the city (or based on the menu or price).

Once the basic questions have been passed (there is still time available?), You can learn more with other questions like:

1. How much do you currently spend and how much have you spent in the past to solve your problem?

Remember to ask the question in the past without getting useless or misleading feedback. Applying the fantastic theory of the ifs, everyone would be willing to spend whatever to solve their problems. But is it really so?

Avoid questions like: "How much would you spend to solve your problem?"

2. Are there other solutions you have tried to solve the problem, if you could tell me about it?

3. Where do you find information about everything that is vegan-friendly?

7 THE PLAN

Let's finally talk about economic resources to finance our project. I promised you it could be done for less than $100. The answer to this challenge is very simple: the first 100 dollars are aimed at a different goal than the realization of the project. This objective is to attract investors: it is with the financing of the investors that the real costs for the project will then be sustained. Many people underestimate this thing, but it is not necessary to have economically covered shoulders to complete an idea. On the contrary, we need a good idea (and you will have the experience to see if yours is). Moreover, if there is someone who is willing to believe, and therefore to invest, in your idea, it is a further guarantee that the idea is actually of quality. This first type of financing, aimed at validating the idea and attracting investors, is called bootstrapping.

Bootstrapping means financing the startup with its savings.

In this phase the funding comes from your pockets (bootstrapping), from those of friends and relatives and from that of investors a bit crazy (and particularly risk-loving). The "change" you receive from family, friends and fools, use them to show that you have the potential for growth.

This is the first funding force, the "simplest" and the one that, at least at an early stage, forces you to be careful while keeping the focus on the goal: VALIDATING THE IDEA AND THE MARKET. You have $100 as the maximum threshold and probably, if you work reasonably, going directly to the core of the problems without getting lost in the details, you can get away with much less. Spend little: just what you need to gather the information you need. In most cases only a few tens of dollars are spent, in photocopies and social media. If your idea works and you've collected the data to prove it, you don't have to spend another cent. The numbers of your idea will suffice to guarantee investors that it is convenient for them to finance you.

If the data you collect is not exciting, it means that you still have to gain experience to arrive at a winning idea. You know what your goal is, you just need to find the right way to put it into practice. You have learned to be resilient and it will not be difficult for you to accept this disappointment and continue to grow.

The idea is not so bad. A market seems to be there and now it's not just me saying it, but I have some concrete data in my hand.

At this point it is necessary to give a more solid structure to the project.

The business plan is a real action plan, where the competitors are analyzed, what their characteristics are, a marketing plan is defined, the market is analyzed with the relative market share to be attacked and much more.

All accompanied by a document, the budget, which lenders want to see first-hand and understand what are the business opportunities in relation to the market.

It is important to do the business plan to be clear about the goals you want to achieve and how to reach them. The business plan defines the strategy and the action plan at 1, 3 and sometimes even 5 years.

Very often the business plan is requested by investors or in general in all situations where you want to finance your startup, attract new business partners or new directors.

By saying let's go straight to doing. Many are wondering what a business plan is made of and how to do it.

The business plan consists of 7 parts, including the executive summary.

Compiling it in all its parts requires a considerable commitment, both in terms of time and resources.

Assuming that without a business plan you can't even get close to venture capital, I'll show you a well-structured business plan. Here, in fact, is generally composed of a business plan:

The Executive Summary is a summary of the whole document divided into sub-paragraphs to allow the investor to read fluently

The team is fundamental in a startup and within the business plan it is necessary to make sure to transmit confidence about the startup team. It is useful to explain the history and the track record and show why these people are the most suitable ones to carry out the startup

The product (or service) and the present and future technology. What differentiates your product from that of its competitors? Do you have trademarks or patents? How do you imagine its evolution in the future?

The Market and the Competition, specifically: target market, where the market share in which your project will fit and what the future prospects are analyzed. Usually to do this we use the TAM SAM SOM analysis.

Startups, especially in the initial phase, find themselves having to calculate these indexes by providing an objective evaluation of the potentials that can be realized as well as greater clarity about the accessibility and usability of the market.

This allows partners, collaborators and investors to more reliably assess the capabilities and the future of the structural implementation of the project, making it less risky for these individuals to invest.

The TAM (Total Addressable Market) is the total market available. It is the total demand for a given product or service. Studying and estimating the TAM is the first step for new entrepreneurs to start their own business. It is important to identify it in a concrete way without exaggerating or underestimating, through subjective filters, as it is essential to identify the suitable market with the highest growth potential.

Investors look at the TAM in different ways, those who show interest in the great potential and those with concern because the high value could be a sign of "red ocean", therefore of high competition.

The SAM (Served Available Market) identifies the potentially available market. It is the concrete market opportunity that exists and therefore the part of TAM that could actually be reached as a target with the product or service that you want to launch or that can be reached from a geographical point of view.

The SOM (Serviceable and Obtainable Market) is the market that can actually be obtained; what you will take (hopefully) once your startup is launched. The calculation of the SOM is an estimate that is based on the presence of internal data available, on the study of one's own strengths compared to the competition in sectors such as promotion, sales, prices and much more. Simply stated, the SOM depends on the ability to make the most of the tools available to it. Being an estimate in this case more subjective than the calculation of the previous indexes, remember not to overdo it, it must be credible, better if accompanied by real data.

Having to explain this instrument in an academic way can be heavy and difficult to understand. The best thing is to think by examples.

In order to accurately compile this tool, you need to do market research and collect as much data as possible. The web is full of reports, articles and forums where you can carry out surveys and gather information, so if you are not a skilled navigator, you should be patient.

Let's take a simple example together to understand how this tool works.

Let's assume we want to produce and market a new model of electric toothbrush with new and innovative properties only for the Italian market (to make it shorter) at a price of around $30, average price for this type of product (we assume, for simplicity, that a dollar is worth as much as one euro).

We know that in Italy (60 million inhabitants) 80% of the population owns a toothbrush but 70% of them own an electric toothbrush. With a brief calculation we know that we are in front of a population of 33.6 million people.

We are interested, in this case, to observe the market in terms of turnover, therefore: a person buys an electric toothbrush once a year at a price of $30. We are facing a turnover of around $1 billion a year. This is our TAM.

We realize that for various reasons, in the first year, we are not going to sell the product online but only through physical stores. As our company is located in central Italy, we know that we will most likely be able to attract more customers who are geographically closer to us. We see that in this area there is a 40% of population interested in our product. This means that central Italy will be able to generate a turnover of $300 million. This is the potentially reachable market or our SAM.

How much can we really get these 300 million? Let's suppose that we have made arrangements with a local distributor and we manage to position ourselves in 10 physical stores that each gather around 100,000 people interested in our product. So, we can really say that we can secure a turnover of $30 million which is 10% of the Sam. This is our SOM.

This example, although not exactly exciting, leads to interesting considerations. How much would turnover increase with more store expansion? How much for online sales? An investor could ask the same questions.

With these calculations we are able to make more objective evaluations for the type of project as they are based on realistic data, while the only thing that is not certain is the SOM which, as mentioned above, is calculated on the basis of hypothetical considerations.

The Swot Analysis where you will talk about your strengths and weaknesses, the opportunities and threats you see in your project through a swot analysis. The swot analysis, also known as "SWOT matrix" or "scheme", is a strategic business planning tool. An analysis technique that has existed for over 50 years and is perhaps one of the most shared and transversal business tools. The matrix allows a rapid, complete and concise analysis of a specific business or project. The tool allows to bring to light, analyze and evaluate: Strengths, weaknesses, Opportunities, Threats.

Performing the swot analysis is very simple and does not require special mathematical or economic skills. Essentially it is a real brainstorming applied to the four areas of the matrix with the aim of completely dissecting the possible strengths and weaknesses, opportunities and threats;

In the Marketing Plan you will have to describe how you want to place your product on the market, what the price policy will be, how you will promote it, which acquisition channels you will use and how much you think it will cost you to acquire new customers;

The Financial Economic Plan will contain:

1. Financial strategies;

2. Sales forecast;

3. Staff plan;

4. Budget;

5. Loans and investments;

6. Investments table;

7. Income statement;

8. Balance;

9. Financial statement;

10. Pre money evaluation.

In addition to the business plan, you will also need to develop a pitch deck:

When we talk about pitch in the startup sector, we refer to a brief presentation, which aims to convince a group of investors to finance an entrepreneurial idea.

Let's get to the heart of this guide and discover together how to achieve the perfect pitch.

In startup competition, teams usually illustrate their idea with slides: the document used for the presentation is called a pitch deck.

But how do you make an effective and impactful deck?

Remember that your goal is to capture attention.

When it comes to creating a pitch deck, many believe they need to go into detail and explain every single aspect of their idea, but this is a serious mistake.

There is no pitch that always goes well and on every occasion. It must be customized according to the target audience.

More importantly, "we must never confuse an investor pitch with a sales pitch". Remember that you don't have to talk about your product/service, but about the value your startup will create by solving a particular problem.

You will be neither the first nor the last of the startuppers to present a pitch to convince investors and raise funds. When you participate in a competition you will not be the only one, but in a sense, you will have to look like it.

Don't Write Too Much and Choose Captivating Images. People will remember little or nothing of what they will hear and read, but they will remember much of what they see.

When you create a pitch deck, you can't absolutely ignore the design.

Choosing the right design means choosing:

a suitable font - it is essential to take into account the relevant public, but in general it avoids "fanciful" fonts or the use of multiple fonts;

an animation style - if you use photographs, avoid inserting illustrations and vectors, in order to maintain a coherence of style;

a set of colors - choose colors that are consistent with your brand but avoid unlikely color combinations if you want to impress your audience.

Use a simple and essential structure.

If the goal of the pitch is to capture the attention of your audience, the hardest part is not to "add", but to take away. When they asked Michelangelo how he had been able to make a horse out of a block of marble, he replied: "It is very simple, I have taken away everything that is not a horse!"

Today, one of the most widespread sayings in the startup world is precisely this, "take away everything that is not horse". What does it mean? It means that you have to eliminate the superfluous and leave only the essentials.

"It creates a synthetic and graphically appealing pitch, but without omitting all the elements and paragraphs typical of a pitch". On the web there are thousands of guides to create a pitch deck, but the structure most used in the presentations is probably the one proposed by Guy Kawasaki, chief evangelist of Canva and, previously, of Apple.

Kawasaki suggests ten slides:

Title - In this slide, enter the name of the startup, the name and the job title of the person presenting the pitch, the contacts (email address and mobile).

Problem-Solution - After the introduction, it is necessary to describe the need that your startup goes to satisfy and explain how it intends to satisfy it: first identify the problem, then indicate the solution.

Value proposition - Now that you've indicated YOUR solution to the problem, you need to explain why it's the best possible solution and what the real added value your startup will create.

The "secret sauce" - It speaks of technology, of the innovation that characterizes the solution you offer and that distinguishes it from everything else: this is the "secret sauce" of which Kawasaki speaks. This is a key slide and must be structured to capture the public's attention as much as possible, thus avoiding the insertion of large textual parts and preferring rather graphics or, even better, a demo or a prototype of your product.

Business model - This is also a key slide: you have to explain your business model or, to put it simply, how your customers' money will end up from their pockets to those of your startup. Remember that investors seek economic returns in the medium to long term and if you don't convince them that your startup is able to make money with the solution you offer, you won't even get a cent.

Go-to-market-plan - It's time to illustrate your "action plan" and share the goals of your startup: how do you intend to conquer the market? According to what timing?

Competitor Analysis - Don't make the mistake of thinking that, being a startup, your company has no competitors. In this slide you have to offer a complete overview of the competitors: who they are, what they do and how you plan to face them to win the competitive challenge.

Team - This is the time to present the team, explaining who they are and what their members do. Remember that investors do not fund ideas, but their execution: you must therefore demonstrate that your team members have the skills and experience to transform your project into a real company, perfectly capable of invoicing and generating profits.

Financial forecasts & business metrics - In this slide you have to present the financial forecasts for the next 3 years, also indicating the key business metrics (engagement, active users, conversion rate, etc.) that will allow investors to monitor success or not of your startup.

Talk me about money - Here we are, it's time your investors were waiting: now you have to explain how much money you need and how you intend to spend it to achieve your startup goals. It explains to them what the current status of the startup is, how far the product development is, the expected timing for achieving the set goals, the planning of the financial outgoings.

Preparing the pitch deck for your startup presentation is just the first step.

Remember that slides are not meant to be read, as often happens in events, conferences and, not infrequently, even in startup competition. They only serve as an accompaniment to your speech, to help the audience keep the focus.

But how to set up effective communication for your pitch?

All the great leaders manage to inspire others because they know their deepest motivations. In other words, they know their why and, more importantly, they know how to communicate it.

Adopt A Simple Language: The Public Doesn't Know More Than You!

The secret to making a good pitch is to use simple, clear and understandable language.

The effectiveness of the message you want to convey is influenced by many factors, including the rhythm of the voice.

Another aspect that is often underestimated is the management of pauses and silences, which often seem to make the speaker of the pitch almost uncomfortable.

Don't improvise your speech. Don't think that you just need to have well-made slides, throw your eye away from time to time and speak in front of investors.

Be careful, though: I'm not saying to prepare a written speech to learn by heart, and then "throw it up" like an automaton during the presentation. Instead, prepare a list of the most important points you want to touch in your speech.

Once the set is ready, it's time to try your speech, but don't expect to make the perfect speech the first time. Steve Jobs himself, famous for his memorable and impeccable presentations, spent weeks trying his speech. And if he did it, he seemed almost to have an innate talent ... well, I'd say you should do it too! Consider that it will take at least 5 attempts to arrive at a version that is effective.

The worst mistake that can be made is not giving importance to the form. The substance in a pitch is worth less than the form. Immediately after the presentation or later it is the substance that matters, but the pitch is the first impression.

Be careful though: it's not just about using the right words, but about communicating in the right way. On the one hand you have to know how to modulate the tone of the voice, placing greater or lesser emphasis according to the importance of what you are saying, also because nobody can like flat and monotonous speeches.

On the other hand, it is also a question of standing: during the tests, you learn to manage body movements, because during the presentation you cannot remain rigid and completely still, but you cannot even move continuously or start jumping all the time.

Practicing in public (e.g. asking for support from friends and relatives) is important not only to learn how to manage time (keep in mind that a pitch can last from 10 to 20 minutes or, in the case of an elevator pitch, from 30 seconds to 5 minutes), but to try, as far as possible, to reproduce the context in which you will hold your presentation, so as to learn to manage the pressure and the fear of public speaking.

8 THE BEST PRICE

Certainly, a crucial aspect of this planning phase is the definition of the price of what we offer.

The sale price is a measure of the economic value that must be paid in the exchange of a product or service, or better yet: it is the sum of money offered in exchange for the ownership or use of a good or service.

From the corporate perspective, all the decisions are summarized within the sale price, from those relating to demand, competition and costs.

From the consumer's point of view, price is often represented as an indicator of the value of the product in relation to its benefits. The more the benefit increases compared to the price, the more the perceived value increases (of course the opposite also applies).

An example is that of the happy hour where cocktails are prepared for a specific time slot which are accompanied by a snack at a certain price, included in the sale price. In this way, the perceived value is much higher than in places that do not offer this service.

To be able to fix it, first of all it is necessary to identify an initial price level to be used as a starting point. In this case we have four different approaches:

to the question; to costs; to profits; to the competition.

Each of the aforementioned methods contains different internally and there can often be an overlap between the various orientations which may make it necessary to consider several models simultaneously.

There are several approaches:

The Skimming Price. We refer to the demand component that expresses a strong desire for the product and is willing to pay a higher price. In this way we start from a higher sum and then progressively lower it to satisfy the rest of the buyers.

When is it effective? When there is a sufficient number of potential customers willing to pay a high sum or when there is no possibility for a competitor to enter the market with a similar product at a lower cost and when the customer receives the high price as an indicator of high quality.

In these cases, the conditions occur in particular when there is a patent that suggests uniqueness and value. Example? Most of the mobile phones just launched on the market have high prices which then go down gradually.

By means of the Penetration Price, a low figure is set which allows to reach high market shares in a short time. When is it effective? When the market is sensitive to the selling price, when low prices discourage competition from entering the market but above all when there is the possibility of exploiting economies of scale. The Nintendo DS has used this strategy to compete with Sony's PSP.

Prestige Price: the consumer associates on several occasions the high cost with a high quality. Attention, often those who use this technique can no longer decrease the price because the prestige associated with a product can be a criterion of choice and reducing it can lower the demand instead of increasing. If the cost goes down temporarily (for example in the form of a discount) the feeling of "big deal" comes into play, which is certainly positive, but if one goes too far with the decrease, consumers could question the quality of the product.

Price Lining: products of the same type are offered (based on the variant) at different price levels. It is a tactic often used by retailers and the advantage is linked to greater clarity of the offer by leveraging different preferences with respect to variations or quantities. The best example is that of Mc Donald's which offers menu variants (medium/large) that allow you to choose between different price options not so much based on the variety of the sandwich as on the size of the drink and chips.

The Psychological Price.

We all know it and every time we are unconsciously kidnapped. The very famous, 99cent. Technique which consists in fixing a price of a few dollars or cents below the whole figure. Strange but true, on a sale price of $2.99 the consumer receives the cost closer to 2 than the $3.

Price Objective, a technique that I think is really interesting even if it requires a very thorough study. Canon uses it to sell its cameras. In this case the producer tries to understand what could be the final price that the consumer would be willing to pay to then define the selling price to be paid to the commercial intermediary.

The Bundle Pricing is used very frequently, it is a method that leads to the marketing of two or more products at a single sale price (remember the example of the happy hour?). The method stems from the desire to make consumers perceive a much higher value given by time savings, greater satisfaction and allows creating synergies between multiple companies, reducing costs.

The Mark-Up Standard Method consists of adding a fixed percentage to the cost of all items belonging to a set or category of products. This mark-up must cover the total costs and allow to generate a profit that is typically between 1 and 2% on the value of sales.

The Cost-Plus Method is a variant of the mark-up and consists of adding a specific amount to the total unit cost of production, both as a percentage and as an absolute value. The percentage value is typically used for limited series products or single items, while the fixed value is more common in the case of some professional services.

According to the Objective Profit Method, a sales price is set based on a specific annual profit target in relation to a specific sales volume. Being a mathematical method, the complete formula (from which you will have to derive the price) is:

profit = (price X quantity) - [fixed cost + (variable unit cost x quantity)]

In a strategy of this type, the company is based on the actions and on the prices of the competition that often poses constraints of behavior.

The customary price is used for those products where tradition, the particularity of the sector and various other competitive factors do not allow to take advantage of many degrees of freedom.

The Market Price Based Method is based on the fact that for different products it is difficult to identify a specific or reference market price. Those who dedicate themselves to the choice can often have a subjective idea of the price of the product, precisely a "market price" that is used as a basis to then choose to place themselves at a higher or lower level than the one initially identified.

The Owl Price, that is to fix a price at a lower level than the usual one of a certain product. This tactic is used to attract attention and lead them to view their business. The aim is not so much to increase sales of that product but to attract customers in the hope that they will buy other products.

It can happen that in determining the price of a product or service it is necessary to consider different approaches and strategies. Perhaps in the span of a year most of the methods indicated could be used without having to be compulsorily bound to only one.

An example of overlap could be the willingness to enter a new market initially, with a strategy to then implement a psychological price jointly oriented to profit.

For a startup, these approaches can be fundamental for a first phase of choice. But what then leads to "guessing" the right selling price may depend on a / b testing to be able to subject different consumers to different price levels, gather information and implement the best solution.

Keep this fact in mind: when you go to any store and make a purchase, you often buy a product for its packaging, as it is impossible for you to interact with the product itself. I've already mentioned the concepts of value and perseverance, use them!

9 THE FUNDS

How to finance your own startup is one of the most important problems that afflict founders and co-founders around the world. The good news I want to give, citing what I often hear business angels say is that: "today, there is no shortage of money, but there are no valid startups to invest in". Let's start from the first point: there is money. The bad news is that, if you look at newspaper headlines that talk about startups with millions (especially dollars) of funding, you might believe that the fund-raising process is quick and easy. This is not the case.

To finance a startup there are numerous roads, all with peculiarities, prerogatives, pros and cons that it is good to know and correlate with the stage of the startup. This is a very important aspect to keep in mind: wrong financing could lead to the end of your startup. The timing in managing the financing is fundamental. If you consult an investor too soon, he could, for example, get the wrong idea about you, your team and your product/service (and a wrong first impression we all know is not desirable). Even too fast growth could lead you to game over.

Participating in an acceleration program could be the way to obtain financial and technical support (especially in the initial phase of your startup). The acceleration programs are programs of limited duration (normally from three to six months), in which the startups receive funding, technical support and networks (with the aim of accelerating the process of maturation of the startup). Normally this is done by financing startups with micro-seed capital. The accelerators do nothing for nothing and normally, in exchange for capital, they ask for an equity percentage (normally between 5% and 15%).

While we have the accelerators, which invest directly in startups by participating in capital, on the other hand we have incubators, which normally do not invest directly but support the startup in "shaping" its business model so that it becomes replicable and scalable. Incubators, normally subsidized publicly or by public universities, work mainly on the idea, trying to build the startup business model (for this reason the incubation program has longer times than an acceleration program). Sometimes they give access to forms of financing and support startups from a marketing point of view.

The Angel Investors, or Business Angels, are people who have a capital to invest in startup projects that they consider interesting. They usually invest following a "hands-on" approach, e.g. preferring entrepreneurial realities in areas close to their own. The first real external financing for your startup could come with them. The Angel appears, usually, in the initial phase of the project and require a solidity of the already structured entrepreneurial project (they are not friends, relatives or madmen, but businessmen). The positive aspects of the intervention of an Angel investor are different: timing of obtaining a very good loan; usually they not only make money available but also networks and skills and for this reason they prefer a geographical proximity to the startup with respect to their professional or business activity; putting money on you as the first mentors and the first supporters of your business = you are no longer alone. On the other hand, the Angel guarantee (normally) limited investments, which often take place in a context of "weakness of the startup" (so the rules of the game are usually decided by them...). In fact, they usually invest sums of money that can range from a few thousand dollars to around $100,000. Normally, Angel Investors finance more than one startup at the same time (knowing that 90% of them will not guarantee a return, they must balance the 9 bankruptcies with the tenth startup that will allow them to recover the invested capital and also earn something). What do these external investors value? Remember the three T: Team rule; Traction; Technology. The idea itself is of little value. The team (if you're not the only performer) is worth a lot. Is your team such that it instills confidence in an investor? The second T is the traction, or the proven proof that there is someone potentially willing to pay for your product/service. You have to entice the investor, make him understand that the market is there and that you have validated the idea (so to do this you had to spend your initial money). The third T is technology. Have you developed a highly innovative technology that gives you a huge competitive advantage over the current market? Well, it certainly won't go unnoticed in the eyes of an investor. It's not necessary, but if there's technology, it's good to take advantage of it.

The exit strategy of the Angel investor follows that of the startup itself, but sometimes they can even get out of the investment at the entrance of an institutional investor (such as a venture capital fund) willing to take Angel shares to increase their own. To evaluate an Angel investor, it is important to understand if the person can "replicate" the investment in a subsequent round. This is seen as an important sign of trust for other institutional investors. Recently Angel investors are increasingly organizing themselves into groups, so-called "business Angel networks": this allows them to share the search for new investment opportunities, increase the amount of funds available to invest and increase the level of skills and network that is destined to startups in which they decide to invest. If you are looking for networks of business Angels in your city, if they are present it is relatively easy to find them on Google by entering "business angels + city name".

When it comes to financing, one cannot but think of banks. This is a little less true for startups. Getting finance from a bank is not a simple thing. It is worth mentioning the world of banks, associating it mostly to the possibility of obtaining personal loans, is useful in the early stages.

Competitions are a great way to "test" the value of your startup and create a network (is there a better opportunity to get noticed by Business Angels, potential mentors or possible collaborators?).

The good placement or the victory in a competition also allows, often, to feed one's startup with capital. The competitions are not only promoted by public bodies, but thanks to the spread of open innovation, there are more and more multinationals and large companies launching their own competitions.

Crowdfunding is nothing more than the collective financing of your startup. A group of people invest their money to support your entrepreneurial effort. It is a good method of financing both in the initial phase and in the growth phase. It also allows you to make your product/service known (acquiring customers and visibility). The cons certainly concern the costs of launching a crowdfunding campaign as well as the return that must be guaranteed to investors (shares in the case of equity crowdfunding or products/services in the event of a reward. In short: nobody does anything for nothing).

Here are the first real "steroids" of growth. Venture capitalists invest large sums in high-risk projects, they are usually financial companies that specialize in investing in risk capital. The use of a venture capital by a startup guarantees extensive (often international) networks, knowledge and (obviously) money. Both Venture Capital and Angel businesses often fill operational gaps found in startups (lack of a network, lack of business experience, lack of fiscal and legal support). This, combined with the vertical skills of the startuppers, creates an excellent substrate for the growth of the startup.

But then what are the negative aspects? One in particular: The greater the injection of money and skills, the greater the loss of control over your startup. Without big words you risk not being the masters of the company you have created. Getting a loan from a VC is not an easy thing (less than 5% of the business plans get a loan). Normally the process of approach and verification adopted by the VCs is the following: 1) Analysis of the business plans (first review) with elimination of the faulty/not promising/undeveloped/non-compliant deal with the internal evaluation criteria (the quantity of the Business Plan discarded is very high at this stage); 2) In-depth analysis of business plans (second review) with verification of the most citric assumptions and maturity of business plan development. Request for supplementary documentation in support of the hypotheses made (the level of the rejected Business Plans is lower than in the first phase); 3) Due diligence with closing of the deal (entry as financial partner, etc.). The methods with which a startup is evaluated by VCs (value analysis) are different. Among the most popular are the multiples method and the analysis of cash flows. The post-analysis value obtained is the negotiating value with which the VCs determine the equity to be requested in exchange for the capital made available. What does a Venture Capital company expect from its portfolio? 60% of startups will fail or will not develop - 30% of startups in the portfolio will make 2-4x in 4-7 years - 10% will be a great success (with returns over 10x).

Once your startup has reached your famous goal, the exit phase will have been reached. Exit is the moment in which the whole chain linked to the startup receives value. The exit is the main objective of those who invest in startups but it is also the goal of entrepreneurs (serial and non-serial). The exit determines the passage from the state of startup to another phase.

The main, not unique, options for exit are:

IPO: Through the IPO the startup makes its actions available to the public. The entrepreneur shares his business to quickly access necessary development funds. And it does so at the end of the "metamorphosis" from idea to enterprise.

Acquisition: the startup is acquired by another company.

Buyback: in this case the founders repurchase the shares of the startup that they had previously sold to the investors.

Remember that unlike the others, you did not start from nothing. You built your functional experience to control your idea. It's true: those who fail are many more than those who succeed. If you fail you will see failure as something educational and functional to a more adequate preparation and sooner or later your success is inevitable, like a mathematical theorem. Congratulations.

I would appreciate it if you leave a review of this book on Amazon or wherever you got it. Thanks!

www.ingramcontent.com/pod-product-compliance
Lightning Source LLC
Chambersburg PA
CBHW020559220526
45463CB00006B/2368